HOME GROWN

Handbook for Christian Parenting

111 Real-Life Questions and Answers

Karen DeBoer

Printed in the United States of America.

We welcome your comments. Call us at 1-800-333-8300 or e-mail us at editors@faithaliveresources.org.

Library of Congress Cataloging-in-Publication Data
DeBoer, Karen.
    Home grown handbook for Christian parenting:
    111 real-life questions and answers / Karen DeBoer.
        p. cm.
    Includes bibliographical references and index.
    ISBN 978-1-59255-491-1
    1. Child rearing—Religious aspects—Christianity—
    Miscellanea. I. Title.
    BV4529.D45 2010
     248.8'45—dc22
    2010030450

10 9 8 7 6 5 4 3 2 1

Mixed Sources
Product group from well-managed forests, controlled sources and recycled wood or fiber
www.fsc.org   Cert no. SCS-COC-002464
©1996 Forest Stewardship Council
FSC

CONTENTS

INTRODUCTION

When I became a parent, my friend Della gave me a copy of the book *Dr. Spock's Baby and Child Care.* Considered radical when it was first published in 1946, the book has sold more than 50 million copies. It was the "parenting bible" for Della's mother and mine. Like them, I used the book religiously, referencing it when I suspected Steph had chicken pox, wanted Sam to quit sucking her thumb, refused to believe it was normal for Kailey to stop napping, and wondered if Tara had colic.

I loved that the book didn't have to be read in one sitting (I don't think I've sat for more than 15 minutes at a time in the 21 years since I became a parent). I also appreciated the excellent index that allowed me to find the exact answer to things I was wondering about. The only thing that seemed to be missing from Spock's book were answers to questions I had about how to raise my children to know God—questions like What does baptism really mean? How should we celebrate Christmas? Is it OK for my child to experience doubt? What if my child doesn't want to go to church?

The book you're holding in your hands is filled with those kinds of questions. Some of them are questions you might have been wondering about for a while. Others you might not think about until your child is older or there's a transition in your lives. For the answers, I consulted a variety of experts: pastors, professors, counselors, theologians, parents, grandparents and more. You'll find their biographies beginning on page 207 and their thoughtful insights scattered throughout the book.

You can read it all in one sitting or use it as I used Dr. Spock's book: checking the index whenever you have a question about something. If you'd like to connect with other parents to swap stories, share ideas, and support each other in the faith nurture of your kids, Patricia Nederveld has written an excellent study guide to accompany this handbook. It offers a series of small group sessions designed for busy parents just like you. Check it out at www.FaithAliveResources.org.

God—the only perfect Parent—has planted the seeds of faith in your children. You get to nurture those seeds and watch their faith grow. This book is designed to provide you with helpful information and hopeful inspiration along the way.

Blessings,
Karen DeBoer

CHAPTER 1

HOME IS
WHERE THE HEART IS

My first (and last) attempt at embroidery was a "Home Is Where the Heart Is" pillow I worked on for a home economics assignment. I quit cross-stitching after "H-o-m," then paid a crafty friend to finish the project. At 15 I knew the value of outsourcing, and I still do.

My kids learned to swim from a certified instructor. They take piano lessons from a professional musician and learn to play basketball from an outstanding coach. As a parent I take full advantage of outsourcing when it comes to teaching my kids.

Seeking experts when it comes to training our kids is a good idea when it comes to swimming, piano, basketball, and even embroidery. Those are specific skills that may be better taught by someone with a certain level of expertise. So, given the value of outsourcing, it just makes sense that when we want our kids to learn about God, we should send them to the best children's ministry program we can find, right?

Wrong. When it comes to faith nurture, studies repeatedly reveal that the primary place children learn about faith is in the home (after all, that's where their hearts are). As a parent—no matter where you are on your personal faith journey—*you* are the biggest influence in the faith development of your child. While your church family may provide all sorts of wonderful children's ministry resources, your kids take their most important cues from you.

God calls parents to nurture the faith of their children and lays out a plan for doing so in Deuteronomy 6. We're to make God part of our daily family routines: walking, sitting, talking, driving, working, thinking, getting up and going. Our homes need to be places where we live as though our mailbox were engraved with the words, "God lives here." When our

Most Significant Religious Influences	Percent Choosing as One of Top 5							
	Grade						Gender	
	7th	8th	9th	10th	11th	12th	M	F
Mother	87	75	77	72	75	75	81	74
Father	64	51	55	49	57	51	61	50
Grandparent	36	28	29	34	27	22	30	29
Another relative	11	12	14	16	12	7	13	12
Siblings	22	14	13	13	15	14	18	14
Friends	22	24	28	25	31	31	22	29
Pastor	60	56	49	45	35	49	57	44
Church camp	23	30	26	25	23	23	20	28
Movie/music star	3	3	4	4	2	2	4	3
Christian education at my church	23	30	25	25	31	25	26	26
Church school teacher	29	27	17	23	20	23	26	21
Youth group at my church	25	25	32	33	33	34	30	30
Youth group leader at my church	13	11	20	17	17	15	15	16
Youth group outside my church	3	6	2	3	4	5	4	4
Youth group leader outside my church	2	1	1	3	4	4	2	3
The Bible	25	30	27	23	16	26	24	25
Other books I have read	2	3	4	4	3	4	3	4
Prayer or meditation	9	15	15	16	20	18	11	19
School teacher	3	5	2	2	3	6	3	4

Most Significant Religious Influences	Percent Choosing as One of Top 5							
	Grade						Gender	
	7th	8th	9th	10th	11th	12th	M	F
Revivals or rallies	3	3	4	4	5	4	3	4
TV or radio evangelist	2	*	1	*	*	*	1	1
Worship services at church	10	10	10	16	14	15	12	13
God in my life	3	3	11	11	13	13	8	13
Work camp	*	1	4	2	5	5	3	3
Mission study tour	0	0	*	0	1	1	*	*
Retreats	7	12	16	20	17	18	11	17
Coach	2	2	3	3	4	4	4	2
Choir or music at church	11	12	8	9	11	6	7	12

*Included mainline Protestant youth only (CC, ELCA, PCUSA, UCC, UMC) weighted by congregational and denomination size.

—reprinted with permission from *Effective Christian Education: A National Study of Protestant Congregations*. © 1990 by Search Institute SM. Used by permission. No other use is permitted without prior permission from Search Institute, 615 First Avenue NE, Minneapolis, MN 55413; www.search-institute.org.

kids wonder about God, we're to share the stories about what God did and is doing and has promised to do. Why? Because they're God's love stories—stories that include us.

> Love GOD, your God, with your whole heart:
> love him with all that's in you, love him with all
> you've got!
>
> Write these commandments that I've given you
> today on your hearts. Get them inside of you
> and then get them inside your children. Talk
> about them wherever you are, sitting at home
> or walking in the street; talk about them from
> the time you get up in the morning to when you
> fall into bed at night. Tie them on your hands
> and foreheads as a reminder; inscribe them on
> the doorposts of your homes and on your city
> gates. . . .
>
> —Deuteronomy 6:5-9 *(The Message)*

God has "outsourced" the faith nurture of children to parents in partnership with the church, and that outsourcing begins at home.

Questions

1. What does the Bible say about parenting?

Although there's not a book of the Bible titled *Everything You Need to Know to Raise Perfect Kids* (trust me, I've checked), the Bible does teach us a thing or two about God's plan for parenting. As Leonard Vander Zee points out, having children has always been part of God's plan for people. Adam wasn't meant to be alone, and neither were Adam and Eve. In fact, in Genesis 1:28, "God blessed them and said, 'Have children and increase in numbers'" (NIrV).

The Bible also assures us that we're not in this alone. In Genesis 17 God meets with Abraham and gives him a covenant promise to be God to him and to his children. That promise holds true for us as believing parents too!

God calls us to participate in that covenantal promise by teaching our children vital faith and godly wisdom as we talk to them about God in the midst of everyday life (Deut. 6:7). The vital faith we're called to share involves more than imparting knowledge; it's living into God's story and developing spiritual practices—prayer, hospitality, forgiveness, and so on—that meld faith to practical living. And when it comes to the practicalities of parenthood, the book of Proverbs reminds us that parenting requires both loving discipline and strong encouragement.

While the Bible *isn't* filled with tips for perfect parenting, it *is* full of imperfect parents. Although Noah, Rebekah, and David provide just a few of the many examples of how not to raise children, the grace God offers those parents provides us with a wonderful example of the kind of love we're called to show our own children: the patient, kind, unfailing, joyful, protecting, slow-to-anger, never-giving-up kind of love that Paul describes in 1 Corinthians 13. And when you fall short of showing that kind of love—as all parents do—isn't it great to remember the assurance that we're not in this alone?

2. Do I need a theology degree to raise Christian kids?

No! While raising kids to love the Lord doesn't require spending time and money on seminary training, it does require spending time with God and investing energy in sharing your faith with your kids. That kind of education happens in your home every day, so here's what you need to know and do:

- Pray with and for your kids. Job did this by getting up every morning and offering God a burnt sacrifice for his kids. As a modern-day parent I've frequently offered my kids burnt toast, but that's not the same thing! Asking God for wisdom as a parent and for a blessing on the lives of your kids is something that should be on your daily breakfast menu.

- Read the Bible to and with your kids and on your own. Many studies show Bible reading to be one of the most significant factors in spiritual growth for adults and kids alike.

- Wonder about God together. It's OK not to know all the answers, but it's important to ask the questions.

- Be part of a church family. Let others share their spiritual strengths with your kids.

- Make God part of your daily routine. Through words and deeds both inside and outside your home, share your conviction that Jesus is Lord.

- Talk about it! Share your own faith experiences with your children.

- Live it! Your kids are watching what you do more than they are listening to what you say.

3. Is it fair to impose my faith on my child?

Passing on your faith isn't an imposition, it's a gift. In fact, when faith is a central part of your life, shaping what you say and do, it's impossible not to share it with your children. As Celaine Bouma-Prediger points out, as Christian parents we want to share our faith because those beliefs—like our children—are so important to us. True faith in Christ can never really be imposed on anyone. We share our faith in the hope that one day our children will decide to make that faith their own.

4. What does it mean to nurture my child's faith? How do I do that?

My father's family owned a bakery. As a child I'd watch my grandfather use one hand to crack dozens of eggs and then add them to a huge mixing bowl filled with flour, sugar, and butter. Although my dad would sometimes let me toss in a handful of raisins or currants, I knew that blending in the yeast was his job. After all, the yeast was the most important ingredient—it activated the dough and made it grow.

Nurturing faith is a lot like blending yeast. Karen-Marie Yust explains it like this:

Faith is a gift from God that lies dormant in children unless and until it is stirred up in them. It is like the yeast that bakers mix into bread: inactive until the baker adds a little warm water and begins kneading to spread the yeast throughout the dough. As parents, we can provide children with a rich spiritual environment that activates their faith and mixes it into their everyday lives.

Think of nurturing children's faith as a process of raising a bicultural child: we want our little ones to know the language, customs, and practices of popular culture—at least in its best forms—and also the vocabulary, rituals, and practices of our faith tradition. Children are exposed to popular culture most of their waking hours; if they are to truly embrace their faith tradition as a second cultural identity, they need to spend much more time exposed to the signs and sounds of faith than an hour or two on Sunday morning can provide. Viewing our homes as places where we can create a spiritual world for children to inhabit alongside their popular culture world helps them discover their religious identity and practice negotiating between the two cultures as God's gift of faith transforms their lives as surely as yeast makes a loaf of bread rise.

> Parents have the awesome privilege of being "God's love with skin on" for their children.
>
> —Scottie May et al. in *Children Matter*, Eerdmans 2005, p. 153

My love for baking was nurtured both in the hours I spent at my grandfather's bakery, immersed in the aroma of yeast, and through my relationships with family members who worked there. The way you and your child "do life" together is what has the most significant influence on how faith is nurtured.

5. How do I surround my child with people who will help me nurture faith?

When it comes to nurturing the faith of your child, it really does "take a village." Helping your child form an identity as a member of God's family means surrounding him with people who will share faith stories, offer encouragement, and show that he is a valued member of a faith community. Here are some ideas to help you make those important connections:

- Attend weekly worship with your child at a church where kids are welcomed and valued. Introduce your child to the pastor and leadership team.

- Participate in church potlucks, picnics, and other intergenerational events. These informal gatherings offer great opportunities for your child to connect personally with the people he sees in church each week.

- Invite to your home your child's nursery care-givers, Sunday school teachers, other children's ministry leaders, and other church members whom your child respects. It's amazing how making an informal connection at home lends itself to further opportunities to connect at church and in other contexts.

- Spend time with believing family members who can model and share their faith with your child. If you live far from family or if family members don't share your faith, Joyce Borger suggests that you "adopt" grandparents, uncles, and aunts who share your spiritual values and will love your child and encourage him or her spiritually.

- Join or start an intergenerational small group in which believers of all ages can gather to learn about God while sharing their faith and encouraging each other.

6. How do I make my home a spiritual environment?

Chances are, along with identifying you as "Mommy" or "Daddy" and being able to pick her "blankie" out of a laundry pile, your child also knows the difference between Mickey Mouse and Thomas the Tank Engine, is able to point to a teddy bear in a picture book, and can recognize the McDonald's logo when you're driving through town. In her book *Real Kids, Real Faith*, Karen-Marie Yust says that in order for your child to relate to and become familiar with biblical characters and images, she needs to experience them the same way that she experiences Mickey and the gang: as part of her everyday world.

Along with the usual childhood toys, books, and music that fill your home, Yust says it's important to add "family prayers, storybooks about Bible characters, music with themes of faith and integrity, images by religious artists, toys and puzzles with religious connections, and family service projects." Making biblical characters and images a natural part of your child's daily life is an important way to turn your home into a spiritual environment.

7. Why take my child to church when she's just a baby?

Our daughter Steph was six weeks old when, dressed in a Boston Bruins jersey, she watched her first hockey game on TV with her dad. Ron knew that she was too young to understand the intricacies of the game, but he wanted to expose her to something that mattered to him, in the hope that one day she'd share that passion.

Although your baby can't engage in a discussion about the fine points of the sermon or offer an opinion on the wall mural in the nursery, exposing her to the sights, sounds, and people at church develops her understanding of church as a place to worship God with her "extended family." It also gives her the opportunity to connect with members of her church family while giving them the chance to know her too.

Ron dressed Steph in Bruins gear and introduced her to the game he loves. Bringing your baby to church is a wonderful way for you to introduce your child to God.

8. Proverbs 22:6 says, "Train a child in the way he should go, and when he is old he will not turn from it" (NIV). What does that mean?

Contrary to popular belief, this text wasn't written to instill fear and future guilt into the hearts of believing parents. It was meant to provide them with an encouraging "rule of thumb." Robert DeMoor explains it this way:

Proverbs provides general insights into the way God keeps creation in his providential care and how, by being wise in living in harmony with those ways, we can live better, more fruitful, and enjoyable lives. As Proverbs 22:6 observes, God made it so that what and how children are taught at an early age shapes them for the rest of their lives—something that modern neuropsychology also observes. It's wise to teach your children to trust and obey God when they're little, because, as a rule of thumb, when you do, they will "not turn from it" when they grow up.

The reason they truly can't depart from it is that what you've taught them goes with them wherever they go and whatever they do. DeMoor also points out that because this proverb is a general rule of thumb, you can't argue backwards and say that if a child does depart from God's ways when she grows up, it's because the parents didn't teach her the right way.

The hope-filled news for us as parents is that even if our kids grow up and choose to live contrary to what they've learned, the things we've taught them are still there in their heads and their hearts. The rest is between them and God.

9. What's the big deal about baptism?

It's hard to imagine that the amazing child in your arms is sinful. Sure, he cries, spits up, and occasionally smells really bad—but *sinful*? Fact is, the apostle Paul included Junior when he wrote, "[. . .] for all have sinned and fall short of the glory of God; they are now justified by his grace as a gift, through the redemption that is in Jesus Christ" (Rom. 3:23-24). Your child was born sin-filled like the rest of us, and has the same opportunity to be freed from paying an eternal price for sin.

While baptism is not a "free pass" to eternity—your child will one day have to make his own commitment to God—it is the declaration that your child's sin is covered by Christ's sacrifice on the cross. At baptism, God, who knew and loved your child before he was even conceived (Jer. 1:5) promises to include your child in his covenant of grace (Gen. 17:7). As an acknowledgment of that covenant, you commit to nurturing the faith of your child. That promise and that commitment is a big deal! So is the promise from the rest of your church family to help.

10. Why do we baptize infants instead of waiting until they are adults?

As Reformed Christians we believe that God's covenant includes children. Leonard Vander Zee offers these two examples from Scripture to help explain why:

> It's clear from the Old Testament that male children were circumcised as infants, including Jesus. Circumcision was a "sign and seal" for the Old Testament people of God of membership in God's covenant. Since, in our view, baptism replaces circumcision as the covenant sign (Col. 2: 11-12), infants should also be baptized.
>
> At the end of Peter's wonderful Pentecost sermon, he calls his listeners to repentance and baptism by saying, "[God's covenant promise] is for you and your children . . . " (Acts 2:39). As the story continues, we hear of several new believers who are baptized with their entire "household." This doesn't prove infants were baptized, but it points to the typical Jewish thinking that children are included in the covenant promise.
>
> Beyond all that, infant baptism showcases God's grace in loving and choosing us before we make any choices ourselves.

How wonderful to be assured of—and to publicly acknowledge—God's grace in the life of your child!

11. What's the difference between infant baptism and infant dedication?

If you compared pictures of a baby's baptism with that of a baby's dedication, you might conclude that the biggest difference is the water or lack of water. In reality, the difference is more about what *God* does than what the parent(s) and pastor are doing.

At a dedication, parents do the action: they present their children to God, commit to be godly parents, and promise to raise the child in God's ways. In baptism, while parents are active participants, God is the main actor, publicly declaring "You are my child" and promising "I will be your God."

Joyce Borger says that if you think of this in terms of directional arrows, dedication is ↑ and baptism is ↓ .

12. Does baptism come with a guarantee of salvation?

Choosing a name for your baby is a big deal. Names help shape our child's identity, so we want to get them just right. I always spent hours poring over long lists of baby names with the pressure of Proverbs 22:1 ("A good name is more desirable than riches") swirling around in my head. My husband participated too, shaking his head "no" at anything exotic, old-fashioned, or likely to make his brothers poke fun.

Joyce Borger says that baptism forms our identity in a way that's like what happens when we give our child a name. Although the name doesn't mean anything to the baby at first, as she hears it over and over again she starts to identify herself with that name. As your child gets older, she will also start to understand what it means to be part of the family with whom she shares a name.

As a family member your child gets to participate in the celebrations and traditions your family observes. He or she will also be given certain responsibilities. All of this helps shape your child's identity.

While it's not something Christian parents want to think about, it's possible that your child will one day reject that family identity. Borger says, "So it is with becoming a part of God's family through baptism. The child is given certain privileges (worship, church education) as well as responsibilities (share the gospel, learn, serve), but it doesn't guarantee that the child will choose to remain a part of God's family."

13. What is God's role in baptism?

When Jesus was baptized in the Jordan River by his cousin John, God opened the heavens and declared, "This is my Son, whom I love, with him I am well pleased" (Matt. 3:17, NIV). God makes that same claim for your child! As Joyce Borger puts it, "In baptism God is making a public declaration that the child being baptized is loved by him, belongs to him and is part of the community of faith. In essence, God is giving this child his or her primary identity."

14. As a parent, what's my role in baptism?

Getting to church on baptism day is the short-term commitment; the rest of your responsibilities involve a lifetime promise. After God declares his love for your child and claims your child as a member of God's family, you get to respond by promising to take a lead role in nurturing the faith of your child and in helping him form an identity as a child of God.

15. What comes after baptism?

Two things come after baptism. The first usually involves a celebration meal eaten with family and friends. The second takes more time—a lifetime, to be exact—as you begin to live out the promise you made to raise Junior to know God. You need to actively seek ways to make God part of your child's daily life. Here are a few ways to do that:

- Starting when your child is small, listen to music that glorifies God, and sing together. **Tip:** Bible verses set to music make memorization fun and easy. (See p. 159 for some great resources.)

- As your child begins to speak, encourage her to put her hands together and say "Amen" as part of your before/after meal ritual. Add words like "I love you, Jesus!" or "'Thank you for bananas, God!" as language skills develop.

- Buy or borrow children's picture Bibles. (See recommended resource list on p. 115 for some suggestions.)

- Include God in your conversations: "Thank you for the sunshine, God," "Look at the pretty flowers God made," "God sure gave you strong legs for jumping!"

- Make attending worship services part of your weekly routine.

- Connect with other believing families in your church to support and encourage each other.

- Start family traditions that bring you closer to God (see p. 108).

- Engage in practical acts of service with your child (see p. 180).

- Parent with the same love and grace that God shows us. (You'll get more ideas on how to do that as you read this book.)

16. How can baptism be made meaningful to my child as he grows up?

When my kids were baptized, photographing or filming the ceremony was seen as a distraction and was frowned upon. As a result, although my kids have video footage of birthday celebrations, the opening of Christmas presents, and their soccer championships, all that marks their baptism is a photo of them beside a special cake! Your child's baptism is an incredibly important milestone of faith. Arranging for someone to discreetly photograph or film your child's baptism is one way to remember that event together.

Here are some other ideas:

- Tell your child the story of his or her baptism. A great time to do this is after witnessing the baptism of someone else. Point out that God didn't wait until that person was an adult to invite him or her into God's family, and emphasize that babies and older children are part of God's family too.

- If your child has believing grandparents (or if you've asked someone to serve as a godparent or mentor to your child), invite them to write your child a personal letter welcoming him or her to the family of God and sharing what God has meant in their lives. Take the letter out and read it together on the anniversary of your child's baptism.

- Create a baptism book or dedicate some pages in your child's photo album to the baptism event. Include pictures of the baptism, the pastor who performed it, and your celebration with family and friends. Also consider including the baptismal certificate and letters written by yourself and others to welcome your child to the family of God. **Tip:** Give family and friends small index cards on which they can write a prayer, a favorite Bible verse, or a simple blessing for your child.

- Mark the anniversary of your child's baptism on your family calendar each year and light a candle to celebrate it.

- Read a special book each year on that date. It could be the baptism book, photo album pages, or a special picture book. Some great choices are *Water, Come Down!* by Walter Wangerin and *Just In Case You Ever Wonder* by Max Lucado.

17. How can I bless my child?

I wonder if Jesus flashed a mile-wide smile after hearing the heavenly blessing from his Dad on baptism day (Mark 1:11). Although our kids aren't waiting for us to part the sky and send down a dove, they do want our blessing. Here are some simple ways you can be intentional about providing it.

Show it. A smile, a shoulder squeeze, a warm hug, and a high-five are all important ways to physically demonstrate your love. John Trent (*The 2 Degree Difference: How Little Things Can Change Everything*) describes how simply lifting your eyebrows and brightening your eyes when your child walks into the room sends a warm "I'm happy to see you!" message and is a powerful way to let him know you value his presence.

Say it. Praise your child for who she is and recognize what she does with simple sentences like "That's a great idea!" or "You're such a great helper!" Make the words "I love you" part of your daily vocabulary. Mark Holmen (*Faith Begins at Home*) also shares a biblical blessing each night with his daughter, using the words of Numbers 6:24-26. Consider adding a biblical blessing to your nighttime ritual or inscribing it on a card. This blessing could be as simple as "God bless you" or "God loves you."

Write it. Pick up a pen and praise your child in a note, then stick it on the bathroom mirror. Slip a "Have a great game" card into a lunch bag or text an "I'm so proud of you!" message when there's something to celebrate.

18. What's a family mission statement? How do we make one?

While raising a family may feel more like managing a nonprofit organization than a Fortune 500 company, there is one thing you can learn from both business models: the value of developing a mission statement to help clarify your goals and keep your family on the right track. A family mission statement is an expression of your family's goals and values as you seek to love and honor God together. Making one can serve as a great reminder that there's more to family life than housework, homework, and extracurricular activities.

You can create a family mission statement any time. Writing one when your kids are small will help you stay focused on raising a family in a way that pleases and glorifies God now. As your kids get older, you'll want to seek their input as you reshape the statement. **Tip:** New Year's Day or the start of a new school year are great times to do this together!

A good way to begin is by asking, "What kind of a family does God want us to be?" and listing ideas. There is no right or wrong way to write a family mission statement. Yours could be a one-sentence motto such as "As a family we seek to love and honor God in all that we do" or a list that begins like this:

As a family we will

. . . love and honor God at home, at school, and in our community.

. . . be thankful for our blessings and share them with others.

. . . show love to each other by being patient and kind.

. . . read the Bible, pray, and worship God together.

Kids of all ages can participate by sharing ideas, decorating the statement page (or their own copies), and/or creating a picture that shows your family living out one of its goals. **Tip:** Help younger kids remember the statement by using pictures to symbolize certain words. Hang the statement on a wall, on your fridge, near the family calendar, or in another place where you'll be reminded of it often.

> Check out these passages for inspiration as you create your statement: 1 Kings 2:1-4; Joshua 24:15b; Micah 6:8.

19. What's a life verse? Should I give my child one?

My grandmother signed every birthday card she sent me with *Love, Oma—Proverbs 3:5-6.* We never talked about her unique signature, but I always understood that those verses were significant to her and that she wanted them to guide me too. They became our wedding text, words of comfort when our newborn required surgery, and an assurance to share with our kids when they found themselves in scary situations.

A life verse is a Bible verse or passage chosen to serve as a guiding principle for your life and/or as a reminder of God's faithfulness. As adults there may be verses that have been especially significant to us at different times in our lives, or one verse in particular that we have clung to in a variety of situations. You may want to choose a particular verse to serve as a life verse for your child. This can be done when your child is an infant or when your child and you are able to choose a verse that speaks to her particular character traits.

You might include the verse in your child's baby album, read it aloud each year on her baptism anniversary, inscribe it on a piece of jewelry, frame it and hang it in her bedroom, write it in a personal letter to your child, highlight it together when she receives her own Bible, or, like my Oma, add it to birthday and graduation cards.

As your kids get older, encourage them to choose their own life verse—and be sure you share the significance of your own special life verse with them too!

Some popular life verses to consider:

Isaiah 40:31; Proverbs 3:5-6; Isaiah 43:1; Hebrews 10:33; Joshua 1:9

CHAPTER 2

FEARFULLY AND WONDERFULLY MADE

I love this story from Matthew 21:

> *The blind and the lame came to [Jesus] at the temple, and he healed them. But when the chief priests and the teachers of the law saw the wonderful things he did and the children shouting in the temple courts, "Hosanna to the Son of David," they were indignant. "Do you hear what these children are saying?" they asked him. "Yes," replied Jesus, "have you never read, 'From the lips of children and infants you have*

ordained praise'?" And he left them and went out of the city to Bethany, where he spent the night (Matt. 21:14-17).

Isn't it great to know that the children who walked the earth with Jesus ran around noisily in the temple courts? Makes me feel so much better about the chaos my kids create in the halls after church on a Sunday morning! And then there's Jesus' fabulous answer to the annoyed and angry people in charge: "From the lips of children and infants you have ordained praise." Jesus saw past the disorderly conduct of the kids and looked into their hearts. He knew that God built praise into children as part of his elaborate design plan and that they were doing what they were made to do.

When it comes to instilling faith in our kids, we aren't starting from scratch. God knit them together, knows them inside and out, and has a plan for their lives (Ps. 139). As parents, our role is to nurture their faith by immersing them in the love of the inescapable God.

Questions
20. When does my child become a spiritual being?

In Psalm 139 we read that before a child is born, God is at work forming, knitting, and intricately weaving

> O Lord, you have searched me and known me.
> You know when I sit down and when I rise up;
> you discern my thoughts from far away.
> You search out my path and my lying down,
> and are acquainted with all my ways.
> Even before a word is on my tongue,
> O Lord, you know it completely.
> You hem me in, behind and before,
> and lay your hand upon me.
> Such knowledge is too wonderful for me;
> it is so high that I cannot attain it.
>
> For it was you who formed my inward parts;
> you knit me together in my mother's womb.
> I praise you, for I am fearfully and wonderfully made.
> Wonderful are your works;
> that I know very well.
>
> —Psalm 139:1-6, 13, 14 (NRSV)

him or her together. Creating your child as a spiritual being is part of God's design. Leonard Vander Zee puts it like this: "A spiritual being is one who is capable of knowing or relating to God. (Actually building that relationship is another matter.) As a human being, a child becomes a spiritual being as soon as his existence begins, and perhaps even before in the heart of God."

21. When does faith start to grow?

In *Real Kids, Real Faith*, author Karen-Marie Yust points out that God doesn't wait until we are fully developed to initiate a relationship with us; through grace, God gifts us with faith when we are born. What's so exciting about that? It means our kids are people of faith *now*, not "just potential people of faith in need of further development before they can truly engage in a spiritual life."

Faith starts to grow as it is activated through loving relationships with a parent(s) and significant others and through opportunities to experience God in prayer, in Bible stories, in music, at church, and in the world. The wonderful thing about being God-gifted with faith at birth is that, even when kids grow up in families where there is turmoil or unbelief, God is still present in their lives, and one day they may come to know and experience that presence.

22. How soon should I start talking to my child about God?

Right away! Think of it like this: when your child is a baby you talk to him or her all the time and provide him or her with stimulating toys, books, and music. Although your child is too little to understand your words, doesn't know how to read, and is unable to identify instruments, you know that regular exposure to those things is important. Same goes with leading your little one to God. Talking to God together ("Thank you for the rain, Lord!"), including God in your conversation ("Look at the beautiful flowers that God made!"), reading stories from a children's picture Bible (see resource list on p. 115 for recommendations), and singing and listening to music that glorifies God are all wonderful ways to introduce your child to God.

23. What does my child understand about God and when?

After my grandfather died, I took my 3-year-old daughter Steph to visit my grandmother. Near the chair where Pake, my grandfather, used to sit, Steph found a small box and asked me what was inside. I explained that the box contained the cigars that Pake used to smoke. Steph nodded and said, "But now Pake lives in heaven with Jesus." Then she looked back at the cigar box and added, "He forgot them!"

Your child understands different things about God at different ages. At age 3, Steph believed that after you died you got to live in heaven, Jesus' home, the sort of place where you'd like to bring the things you loved on earth. Her concept of God and heaven weren't unusual for a preschooler. Children grow and develop spiritually just as they do intellectually, physically, and socially. The "Spiritual Characteristics of Children" chart below can provide you with a sense of where your child might be spiritually and the corresponding ways in which you can nurture her faith. Note: Be prepared to have *your* faith nurtured by your *child's* understanding of God too!

Spiritual Characteristics of Children

Preschoolers

- believe that God is real (like a grandpa) and that God lives in heaven or at church.

- sense that God loves them and provides comfort (like their favorite blanket or their parent).

- readily accept what you tell them about God.

Nurture their faith by

- letting them know God loves and cares for them by pointing out examples of that love and care in daily life. For example, say things like "God made your skin all better after you fell on your knee" and "God sure loves to hear your singing!"

- sharing your wonder and awe about who God is and what God has done. For example, say "I wonder how God made so many colors. God is amazing!"

- reading Bible story books together.

- singing and listening to music that glorifies God together.

Five- and six-year-olds

- have a strong sense of who God is and often relate to Jesus as their friend. Can be delighted and awed by Bible stories and use their imaginations to ask questions about the Bible and God.

- are able to express their love for Jesus in their own words and actions.

Nurture their faith by

- helping them sense that they are an important part of God's family, the church. Some examples: Thank your child for teaching you a Sunday school song, include his or her signature on a card for a church family member, encourage your child to personally contribute to the offering.

- inviting them to add their own words when praying together, and encouraging them to talk to God on their own, anytime and anywhere.

- reading Bible stories together and pausing to imagine the sights and sounds and people in the stories. For example, "I wonder what Noah's kids thought when he said they were going to build an ark and sail away" or "I wonder what the shepherds' faces looked like when the angels appeared."

- giving them a variety of opportunities to express their faith. For example, after reading a Bible story together, invite your child to draw, paint, or make a reminder of the story; act out the story for or with you; pray with you; or choose a song to sing.

Seven- and eight-year-olds

- are capable of understanding basic salvation concepts.
- express opinions and feelings about God and church; enjoy asking a great many "why" and "how" questions.
- often include prayer in their daily routines; although their prayers may be self-centered, they're sincere and offered in faith.
- often see issues in black and white, but are aware of the struggle between good and evil in the world and sometimes also in their own lives.

Nurture their faith by

- providing opportunities for them to express their love for Jesus.
- encouraging them to ask questions and to wonder aloud.
- inviting them to share ideas about what and who you could pray for together.
- helping them process their fears and guilt feelings about not living up to God's expectations by reminding them that God is a loving and forgiving God.

Nine- and ten-year olds

- have a strong sense of right, wrong, and fairness. May show an increasing concern about people who are hungry, homeless, or poor.

- are often open to learning about other cultures; are becoming more accepting of differences in others.

- see God as a friend who takes an interest in their life.

Nurture their faith by

- helping them understand that because sin entered the world, things that are "wrong" happen and letting them know that this makes God sad too!

- serving others together.

- exploring God's world by learning about other places and cultures in books and online and experiencing other cultural groups in your community.

- making prayer a natural part of your daily conversations with God while driving to school, going for a walk through the neighborhood, and so on.

Eleven- to thirteen-year-olds

- are developing their own beliefs and values in the context of peers, school, media, and church.
- are quick to point out injustice and eager to make a positive difference in the world.
- admire and seek to imitate adult faith-models as a way of establishing their own identity.
- may have doubts and question their faith (especially as they get older); want to think for themselves, which may mean rejecting a parent's faith.
- may find it difficult to integrate their religious beliefs with their everyday attitudes and behaviors; often feel that living as a Christian is impossible.

Nurture their faith by

- getting involved in active ministry through service projects and looking for ways they can participate in ministries at your church, such as outreach and worship.
- helping them think through moral issues and give reasons for their choices.
- being a faith model to them by sharing your love for the Lord and your confidence in God's faithfulness, demonstrating how your faith affects

your choices, and being honest about times you struggled to understand God and why you continue to believe even when you don't have all the answers.

- having regular devotions together.
- assuring your child that God doesn't expect perfection; God's grace is a gift.

24. When should I begin to nurture the faith of my child?

You began nurturing faith from the moment you and your child first met. Elizabeth Caldwell puts it like this: "When you sing to your newborn son and tenderly hold him as you feed him or meet your adopted daughter for the first time and silently say a prayer of thanksgiving to God for this gift of life, then your nurturing this little one in faith has begun." Through your relationship your child learns about love, trust, acceptance, and forgiveness. That shapes his or her understanding of God's unconditional love, faithfulness, and grace. It's in the ordinary details of everyday life that your child's faith is nurtured and formed.

25. How does my faith impact my child's faith?

On the second day of my teen daughter's part-time job, she encountered a rude customer. After work Sam indignantly told me how demanding the woman had been, ending with, "And she should know better—she's a *mom*!" I've never provided Sam with a list of what it means to be a mom or tested her knowledge of all things motherly, yet a big part of what she understands about motherhood comes from observing me.

Your child learns about faith in much the same way. Elizabeth Caldwell points out that even before kids can speak, they are watching and listening and forming an understanding of what their parents are doing. When you read the Bible, pray, show trust in God, participate at church, or show hospitality to someone in need, you are impacting your child's faith. Likewise, not reading the Bible or praying with your kids, complaining about church, and being more concerned with getting than giving also impact your child's experience of what it means to live faithfully.

Knowing that I have the biggest impact on what Sam understands about motherhood spurs me on to equip myself with the wisdom and experience of other mothers and experts. We need to do the same with our faith! If we are to help our kids develop a rich, lasting faith, we need to develop our own faith by engaging in spiritual practices that deepen our relationship with God. Praying, reading, and studying Scripture; listening to and singing songs and hymns; celebrating the Sabbath; connecting with other believers; and serving in our community are just some of the ways we can nurture our own faith—and the faith of our family.

26. When I mess up will it mess up my child's faith?

There are a multitude of ways we mess up as parents—from forgetting to pack a preschooler's "indoor shoes," to breaking a promise, to missing an important event, to losing your cool when you're running late in the morning. Messing up as parents is inevitable; having our mistakes mess up our child's faith is not. In fact, how we handle our mistakes can reveal something to our kids about God and the building blocks of our faith: confession, repentance and forgiveness. Ron Nydam says,

> Our children learn the most about faith in a forgiving God from how we as parents handle our living, our making mistakes, and our personal shortcomings. . . . If they hear us saying that we are sorry, they will learn the blessing of

apology. If they observe us making amends for a careless word, a short temper, or a thoughtless decision, they will learn firsthand the importance of accountability and respect for others as well as the reality of grace when forgiveness really happens. On the other hand, if our children observe us not acknowledging our own sins, not modeling repentance, they will learn something very different. They will learn that the best way to deal with "messing up" is to avoid it, or minimize it, or even deny it.

We also mess up as Christ-followers, often falling short in our relationship with God. Although you don't need to overwhelm your child with too much information, sharing the times you messed up and experienced God's grace is another important way to model faith in action in a way that helps your child in his or her own walk with God.

27. Is it OK for my child to experience doubt?

Our preschoolers were tentative swimmers, so most summers my husband shivered in the shallow end of the pool, holding his arms out and saying, "Just jump—I *promise* I'll catch you!" until eventually they'd take a leap of faith. After that first fearful jump the same thing always happened: they'd climb back out and joyously jump in over and over again! They had experienced the elation that comes with believing in the face of doubt.

Doubt and faith go together. Your child will have unanswerable questions about the ways of God—just like you do. In his book *Helping Our Children Grow in Faith*, Robert J. Keeley warns that when we oversimplify things and try to explain everything about God to our kids in order to avoid doubts, we risk presenting them with a "watered-down version of God." As Keeley points out, "God did not *intend* for me to be able to figure everything out" (p. 50).

Letting your child know you believe even though you have doubts will *nurture* her faith, not *diminish* it. The key is to wonder honestly along with her ("It *is* hard to believe that the water of the Red Sea turned into a wall long enough for the people to walk through. I wonder what that looked like too")—and to let her see that you've struggled too.

Frederick Buechner says in his book *Wishful Thinking*, "Whether your faith is that there is a God or that there is not a God, if you don't have any doubts, you are either kidding yourself or asleep. Doubts are the ants in the pants of faith. They keep it awake and moving."

Allowing your children to experience doubt nurtures a rich faith that is deep and wide enough to handle the questions that they will inevitably ask—a faith that makes them eager to jump in the pool.

28. What if I don't know all the answers?

When it comes to questions about bedtimes, healthy lunches, and allowances, your kids should think you have all the answers. But when it comes to questions about God, your kids need to know you don't. They also need to know that you believe anyway. In *Helping Our Children Grow in Faith,* author Robert J. Keeley puts it like this: "Letting children see that we don't have it all figured out gives them permission to live with questions at the same time that they hold on to what they do know—that God loves them and that he is holding them in his hand" (p. 58).

29. Should I parent each child the same way?

I once watched three school-age siblings arrive at the beach with their mom. The oldest child placed her towel perfectly on the sand and carefully applied sunscreen. The middle child tossed his towel, kicked off his sandals, and splashed into the water. The youngest child handed his towel to his mom and began crying when he realized no one had brought his beach toys. Three kids, three very different personalities. It's no surprise that parents feel torn between taking a one-size-fits-all approach and tailoring their parenting to each child. Marc Houck suggests approaching this dilemma from a "both/and" rather than an "either/or" perspective by adopting some common principles to guide your parenting and by taking into account the unique needs of individual children.

First, each child needs to experience love through a rich bonding with his or her parent(s). Kind words, encouragement, forgiveness, and an investment of time are all important ways to express that love. In addition, parents need to provide clear limits, guidance, and boundaries for their children. As Houck points out, God regularly demonstrates this parenting technique to us—loving us unconditionally and extending grace and forgiveness while providing us with clear expectations and limits.

Second, parents need to consider the unique temperament, style, passions, and interests of each child; and then match encouragement, discipline, and overall shaping to those unique qualities. As a result, while each child will be parented using common guidelines, each child will also be parented in a different way. For example, while parents must *show* love to each child, they also need to be aware of how each child best *receives* love. While hugs, pats on the back, and other appropriate physical affection may be really important to one child, a sibling may experience love better through verbal praise and encouragement. Same goes with limits and consequences—while a "look" from a parent may be all it takes for one child to change a behavior, a sibling may not be swayed until the parent spells out specific consequences. In both examples the guidelines are the same, but the details of what works best for each child are different.

30. What if my child doesn't turn out the way I hope she will?

My friend Mick always said that his biggest dream for his kids was that they would love God and be happy—everything else was secondary. "Then," he says, "one of them made a life decision I didn't like, and I realized that even though he loved God and was happy, that *wasn't* all I cared about."

According to Marc Houck, all parents have hopes, dreams, and expectations for their children, and that's not a bad thing! Wanting our kids to be the best they can be motivates us to do good things for and with them. In many ways, that reflects what God, our heavenly parent, wants for us.

When kids choose their own path in life—and when that path is very different from the one you'd hoped they would choose—it's important to realize your own boundaries as a parent. It's also important to acknowledge the range of emotions you feel as a result, and to seek support and encouragement in order to move forward. Houck acknowledges that that's easier said than done, but adds, "In the end, it is God who is in charge of our children's life stories. Those stories are ultimately about his story with them, of which we get to be a major part."

The best thing you can do as a parent—no matter which paths your kids choose—is to continue to pray for them, accept what you can't change, and look for enjoyable ways to continue to share your lives with each other.

31. How do I love my child when he doesn't love the things I love?

Nine-year-old Amelia is a fierce competitor on my daughter's basketball team. She's strong, she's fast, and she doesn't like to lose. Her parents never played sports growing up, so when Amelia broached the subject of playing basketball they went online to see what was involved. Since their daughter made the team, they have learned the rules, they've volunteered to make tournament posters, and they cheer wildly whenever Amelia scores a basket. They recognize that part of sharing a life journey with their child means learning about the things that matter to her.

Our kids aren't us. They are their own unique God-creations. Discovering what God created them to do is part of the fun of parenting. So introduce them to the things you love, then stand back and see what happens. If Junior loves hockey as much as you do, great. If not, help him find out about all the other things God intended for him to do. And be sure to cheer him on along the way.

CHAPTER 3

SETTING BOUNDARIES, SHOWING GRACE

P aul makes it all sound so simple with his Ephesians 6 directives to parents ("Don't exasperate your children") and to children ("Do what your parents tell you"). Clearly, Paul never sat at a soccer field with a six-year-old who begged to be signed up for soccer but then refused to play or experienced the stubbornness of a two-year-old determined not to climb into his car seat!

Paul's God-inspired guidelines are great in theory; after all, if parents always took time to gently lead

> Children, obey your parents in the Lord, for this is right. "Honor your father and mother"—which is the first commandment with a promise— "that it may go well with you and that you may enjoy long life on the earth." Fathers, do not exasperate your children; instead, bring them up in the training and instruction of the Lord.
>
> —Ephesians 6:1-4

their kids in God's way and if kids honored their parents with obedience, family life would run much more smoothly. But the guidelines are difficult to observe in practice. Truth is, our kids mess up and so do we. That's what makes parenting (and being a kid!) so challenging. Like our children, we are works in progress. Boundaries will be pushed; expectations will be challenged.

We have much to learn from the role model we and Paul share: the God of grace. As parents we need to extend grace to our kids when they mess up. There are also times when we need to apologize for our less-than-perfect parenting techniques and ask our kids to extend some grace our way. While Paul may not have experienced the challenges of modern parenting, his writings can teach us much about living grace-fully.

Questions
32. What does discipline have to do with my baptism commitments?

Vowing to lovingly raise our child, nurture her faith, and help her form an identity as a child of God seemed like such a simple promise on her baptism day. But three years later when I discovered that same child gleefully ripping up the pages of my prized coffee-table book, those vows weren't the first thing that came to mind as I quickly contemplated discipline strategies!

Celaine Bouma-Prediger connects baptism commitments to discipline decisions like this:

> In the sacrament of baptism, we take vows as parents. These vows are to love the child and to raise him up knowing both our love and God's love for him. The vows and the prayers in this service speak of God's amazing grace, which both cleanses and renews us. It is upon that grace we as parents depend to guide the discipline of our children . . . the children God has graciously given into our care for a time.
>
> We promise to pray for our children and ourselves, asking God to guide us as we train them so that together we can grow in the knowl-

> Over each of my daughters' beds is a picture (made by their great grandmother) which has her name and birthdate, and underneath a poem—"a precious gift from God above, ours to treasure, ours to love." It has served me well to read and remember these words.
>
> —Celaine Bouma-Prediger

edge and understanding of our faith.

We also promise to show in our person as parents the joy of new life in Christ!

These are powerful words that seem to invite both a presence of discipline and mutual learning. The balance we walk is delicate, some days more delicate than others, and for this journey we depend upon God's grace and the wisdom he gives us as parents.

33. How does grace factor into discipline?

Like most parents, when I've been given the opportunity to extend grace to a demanding toddler, an impatient six-year-old, or an impulsive preteen, I've often fallen short. What would Jesus—who regularly extended grace to demanding Pharisees, impatient crowds, and impulsive disciples—do if he were parenting our kids?

When it comes to discipline (and all other areas of parenting) Celaine Bouma-Prediger suggests we follow Christ's example and lead with grace:

Grace inside one's heart as a loving parent will guide the discipline, the choices one must make. To act quickly out of one's own anger or even a sense of what is "right" could damage children's fragile sense of self. We are guardians of their growing selves, caretakers, so to speak. Teaching them how to love, how to get along with others, and how to behave in different situations requires grace and wisdom. (Not to mention patience!)

When you and your child are caught up in conflict, Bouma-Prediger says remembering to pause and take a deep breath before speaking or acting gives you time to settle into a deeper place within, in the hope that what you're about to say or do will be consistent with the heart of God.

34. How does how I was raised impact how I discipline my kids?

Most parents can recall a moment when they surprised themselves by saying or doing something exactly like their own parents did—even though they'd vowed it would never happen. Although it may be surprising *when* it happens, we shouldn't be surprised that it *does* happen—we tend to parent the way we were parented ourselves. Thankfully, according to Marc Houck, even though our default parenting response is impacted by what we experienced as kids, it doesn't have to determine how we discipline our own kids.

If there are patterns in your parenting that you want to change, Houck recommends first considering the rules—both spoken and unspoken—with which you were raised. Identifying and evaluating those rules will help you understand what's been forming the foundation of your own discipline style. The next step is to assess your own parenting systems, to look at what is or isn't working and to determine what you want to change. Finally, Houck suggests sitting down with the other parent (or a trusted friend or parenting coach), making specific plans for change, and outlining ways to determine how well those plans are working.

35. What do I do if my parenting style is different from that of the other parent of my child?

Mom thinks it's important for Junior to help clean up after supper; Dad hated doing chores as a kid and thinks Junior should be able to go outside and play. Guess who Junior looks at as soon as the meal is done?

Inconsistent parenting enables kids to play one parent against the other, creates confusing messages about expectations, and leads to feelings of insecurity. It's important to get on the same page as parents because, as Marc Houck explains, kids feel safest when they know where they stand and tend to do better in an environment where there are consistent expectations. Houck offers the following suggestions to help you make that happen in your home:

- Understand that how you parent is impacted by how you were raised. Discuss the good and the bad about how you were parented, and consider what you would like to keep and what you don't want to repeat. Be humble and willing to compromise and to learn from each other.

- Develop a shared vision and goals for parenting. Some questions you might ask: "What do we want our children to experience in this family? What do we want to communicate to them with our words and actions? What is it that we want for our children?"

- Consider strategies that will help achieve those goals. Houck says some of these strategies may come out of the positive parenting you experienced, some may come from Scripture; others may come from good parenting books and other resources.

It would be nice if we had all our parenting ducks in a row before we became parents—but the reality is that parenting is on-the-job training! And, as parenting expert and author Barbara Coloroso points out in her book *Kids Are Worth It!,* developing a parenting structure together is " . . . not a onetime decision but an ongoing commitment to ourselves and our children." It takes work, time, and practice!

36. There are so many Bible-based parenting methods and approaches. How do I know which one I should use?

A few years ago my friend Annie took a Christian parenting course with several other parents. A big part of their study focused on "God's way" versus the "wrong way" to discipline children. After the course, the families got together to celebrate. During the party some of the kids began fighting and one set of parents told another parent that he wasn't parenting "God's way." Six months after completing the course, none of the participants were speaking to each other.

Although the parenting course didn't cause the friendships to end, the mistaken belief that there is only one way to raise Christian children contributed to their demise. There are many Bible-based parenting courses and methods available, but the truth is that there is no perfect child-raising formula and there is no guarantee that your choice of parenting techniques will produce a godly child.

> Parenting, like all tasks under the sun, is intended as an endeavor of love, risk, perseverance, and, above all, faith. It is faith rather than formula, grace rather than guarantees, steadfastness rather than success that bridges the gap between our own parenting efforts, and what, by God's grace, our children grow up to become.
>
> —Leslie Leyland Fields, "The Myth of the Perfect Parent," *Christianity Today*, January 2010, p. 27. Used by permission.

When searching for a parenting resource, Celaine Bouma-Prediger says it's important to gather suggestions, check out different manuals, and look for one that feels authentic to your faith and reasonable for your life. When choosing a parenting method or approach, she suggests asking yourself the following questions as a tool for evaluation:

- Does it fit with our/my theology of family?

- Does it fit with our/my values and practices?

- Does it suit us as a family unit in terms of temperament and lifestyle?

- Does it work with our/my kids?

37. How do I get my kids to understand why obedience to God's rules is so important?

"Don't talk with your mouth full!" "Don't use your outside voice inside!" "Don't run in the halls!" When you're a kid it seems like rules are designed to slow you down and take away your fun. It's important we show our kids that, unlike the rules whose sole purpose seems to be slowing them down and curbing their fun, God's rules were created with a "soul" purpose—one that allows them to serve God by living a life of obedience to him.

Although "Because I said so" may be an easy way to get your kids to obey and "Because God said so" may scare them into submission for a little while, kids are more likely to follow the rules if they understand the "why" behind them.

Consider together why God's rules make sense. Imagine how life would be different if stealing were OK, or wonder aloud about what would change if everyone in the world loved each other.

Tell your kids that one of the great things about God is that God didn't just leave us a set of rules—he promises to help us obey them! Make asking God for commandment-keeping assistance part of your prayers together.

Finally, remember that your kids are watching to see if your actions match your words, so lead by example. Don't bad-mouth your neighbors. Let the cashier know when you're undercharged. Forgive people who hurt you. Don't ask your kids to say you're not home when you don't want to answer the phone. Spend time with God. If you want your kids to learn it, they need to see you live it.

38. How do I teach my kid to make wise and age-appropriate choices?

When our daughter Steph was four, she used a permanent marker to scribble letters on a lampshade. Although we were angry that she'd ruined the lamp, we were reassured that she'd never have a successful career defacing buildings—the letters she'd scribbled spelled her name.

Coloring on the shade was a poor choice—but not a surprising one given the stage of Steph's brain development. Although she knew she wasn't allowed to color on the furniture, her pride in being able to print her own name and her confidence in her ability as an artist trumped any thought she may have had about getting caught.

Brain development research backs that up. In fact, recent research has proven what parents have always known: that the answer to "What were you thinking?" is "I wasn't."

In her book *What Every 21st-Century Parent Needs to Know,* author Deborah W. Haffner says scientists now know that "the prefrontal cortex, which helps set priorities, organize ideas, and control impulses, is one of the last parts of the brain to mature" (p. 78). As a parent, you can help your child make good choices while his or her brain is a work in progress by

- setting age-appropriate limits and boundaries.
- allowing your child to experience natural consequences for poor choices. (For example, a natural consequence of refusing to wear a jacket to school is being cold at recess.)
- considering what the Bible says about how God wants us to live. (For example, how does God want us to take care of the world and what does that have to do with what we choose to buy?)
- praying with your child when he or she is making a decision about something and letting him or her know that you talk to God about your decisions too.

39. How do I foster an environment of mutual respect?

When our kids were little, one of our favorite after-dinner activities was to crank up the music, pass out wooden spoon "microphones," and perform together. Aretha Franklin's "Respect" was a popular song on our playlist, probably because the kids liked singing "sock it to me" as fast as they could. Although Aretha taught them how to *spell* R-E-S-P-E-C-T, we had to teach them how to *show* respect.

Judy Cook says that when it comes to creating a culture of respect, it's helpful to think of the three levels of a home:

Level 1: Parents

Treat each other with respect. That means no yelling, no put-downs, and no physical violence. It also means affirming each other's differences, supporting each other, and taking co-responsibility for nurturing children. If you are a single parent and the other parent is in the picture, it's important to practice respect when talking about and dealing with that person, especially when your children are in earshot.

Level 2: Children

Treat your children with respect and insist that they be respectful to each other. Set rules related to boundaries. For example, if a child wants to borrow something belonging to a sibling, he or she should ask first. If a child gets angry, require that he or she use words, not fists, to express the anger in an appropriate way.

Level 3: Family

Treat each other with mutual respect. For example, give each other space, share TV or computer time fairly, have mealtime conversations where everyone gets to finish his or her sentences before someone else pipes up.

The key thing to remember is that children learn what they live, so lead by example.

40. Is it OK to be angry with my child?

When you've just discovered your preschooler proudly printing her name in permanent marker on your lampshade, it's hard to remember that as a Christian you're called to be "slow to anger." Judy Bogaart says that as a parent it's OK to feel angry; what's important is how you choose to deal with that feeling. To help with that, Bogaart suggests the following:

- Calm down before handing out consequences. Take a personal "time out" if necessary, and tell your child you will talk about the incident later.

- Acknowledge your feelings. "I think it's great that you know how to print your name, but I'm very angry because marker does not belong on my lampshade."

- Match consequences to the behavior and remember that consequences aren't about retribution but about teaching your child what's important to you: responsibility, loving God and others, respect, and so on. In the case of the lampshade incident, you might say, "I'm going to put away your markers until tomorrow, and we're going to talk about places you may and may not use them."

- Apologize when you've responded inappropriately. "I'm angry that you colored on my lampshade, but I shouldn't have yelled at you. I'm sorry." Demonstrate to your child that while anger can be a valid feeling, losing your temper is not the way to handle it.

41. How do I deal with my anger?

Whether your children are three feet tall or almost taller than you, they know how to push your buttons! Here's what Judy Bogaart suggests you do when one of those buttons is "anger":

- Acknowledge what you are feeling to yourself. Calm your body down with several deep breaths.

- Admit your feelings to your child. "I'm really angry right now. When I'm calm we'll talk about this more."

- Get calm so you can deal with the situation properly. Do something physical like walking or running to release pent-up energy, or do something relaxing like taking a bath. If you're married, you might talk things over with your spouse to get his or her perspective and input.

- Ask yourself, "What is the real issue here for me? Why am I so upset? What would solve this problem for me? How can I best convey my feelings to my child in a way that will impact him and his behavior? Do the consequences I'm considering make sense given the behavior? Will they teach my child what I want him to learn?"

- Come back to the issue when you (and your child) are calm. **Tip:** Sometimes it helps to brainstorm a solution together. "It seems like you have a hard time getting home by 6:00. What do you think would help you get home on time for dinner?" Write down all the ideas that come out of your brainstorming—whether you agree with them or not—then talk about them together, removing those that you or your child can't live with. Choose one solution and try it for six weeks. If it doesn't work, try one of the other ideas.

42. How do I not take it personally when my kids argue back?

Remember two things: (1) it's not about you, and (2) you are the adult. Your kids *are* going to disagree with your decisions and push back against the limits you've established. They naturally desire independence (that's a good thing!), and that means wanting to make their own decisions.

Your job is to remember that it's not personal. While it's never OK for your child to attack you personally (either verbally or physically), when he argues back you need to demonstrate respect as you re-state your points and calmly consider his perspective.

43. What do I do when my child is angry with me?

We should never intentionally provoke our children to anger (Eph. 6:4), but there will be times when they will be angry about what we say or do. Judy Bogaart reminds us to use the times when *we* are angry to model appropriate responses by acknowledging our feelings ("I can't believe I left that book at home—how frustrating! That makes me so angry!"), problem solving ("I guess I'll have to go home and get the book"), not saying things that are hurtful, and taking time out to calm down.

When your child is angry with you, remember not to take it personally, and remember all the times you were angry with her too. Be sure to give her space and time to process her feelings. Let your child know it's all right to feel angry, but it's not OK to be hurtful as a result. Teach kids that they have a choice in how to respond when angry, and provide them with practical ways to calm down.

Some examples: taking several deep breaths (in for four counts, out for eight, repeat three or four times), physically removing themselves from the situation by going to their room or taking a walk or being anywhere else they can safely deal with their feelings.

Encourage your child to try to understand what he is feeling, what the problem is for him, what's needed to feel better, and/or how the problem could be solved. Once your child is calm, be respectful of feelings and needs as you discuss the problem together. (You don't have to do what your child wants, but you do have to listen to him carefully.) Remember that a child learns respect from the way you demonstrate respect to him.

44. How do I teach forgiveness to my child?

I once led a large group of kids in a children's worship time on the theme of forgiveness. At the end I invited them to share prayer requests that connected to the theme. A seven-year-old boy in the back row raised his hand and said, "I'm sorry for hitting my brother on the head with a rock." Before I could respond, the hand of his younger brother shot up from the front row. "I forgive my brother for hitting me with the rock." The glimpse of grace these brothers gave us made extending forgiveness look easy, but we know it's not always that simple.

According to Leonard Vander Zee, "Forgiveness is one of the hardest things to practice in our close relationships." Teach it to your child through demonstration and experience.

Say "I forgive you" when your children say they are sorry—and extend forgiveness even when they don't say it. Demonstrate forgiveness by not holding a grudge and not revisiting the wrong. Note: Forgiving a transgression doesn't always mean eliminating the consequences the transgressor will have to face. Forgiving your child for coloring on the wall doesn't excuse him from cleaning up the damage.

Model forgiveness in your daily dealings with others. Show grace to the cashier who accidentally shortchanged you, the driver who cut you off in traffic, and the neighbor kid who threw a ball through your window.

Encourage empathy. Ask your child to think about a time when she was sorry for the wrong thing she did. How did she feel before and after she was forgiven?

Be realistic in your expectations. Acknowledge your child's hurt feelings and let him know that forgiving doesn't mean forgetting the bad thing happened, and the hurt may take a while to go away. As Vander Zee points out, "Forgiveness remembers and forgives at the same time. But it doesn't remember with bitterness; it remembers with compassion. That's what's so hard about it."

Help your child understand that we all sin, we all make mistakes, and we all need forgiveness—that's why Jesus came.

Be patient. Forgiveness for deep hurts takes time. Encourage your child to talk to God about his or her struggle when it's just too hard to forgive.

45. Should I ever apologize to my child? (And do I really have to make sure that the "sun doesn't go down" before I do?)

All parents make mistakes in the way we deal with and relate to our kids. We become impatient, lose our temper, say or do hurtful things, and sometimes we're just plain wrong. Saying "I'm sorry" to your child is important because it models responsibility, teaches accountability, demonstrates respect, and shows that you aren't perfect.

While it's preferable never to end the day in conflict, there are times when it's better to wait until those involved are calm, can speak respectfully, and are open to listening to each other. When evening comes and you or your child are still too upset to talk about the problem, Judy Bogaart says it's still important for you to connect with your child and assure her of your love—even if that means say-

> Children do not need perfect parents, simply good enough parents. To support our children in their spiritual formation, we simply need to be on the journey with them, learning and growing, willing to say "I'm sorry" and to seek God's transforming grace, love, and strength.
>
> —Scottie May et al., *Children Matter*, Eerdmans 2005, p. 158. Used by permission.

ing "Goodnight, I love you" from outside her closed bedroom door. Your child needs to know that no matter what the conflict, your love for her is unchanged.

46. Should I always make my child say "I'm sorry"?

Forcing your child to apologize when he or she isn't ready feels like a lesson in lying, but skipping the "sorry" seems like a big thumbs-up to bad behavior. The solution: make apologies meaningful by helping your child understand how and why his behavior was wrong:

- Discover the cause. If you weren't present, ask: "What happened that led you to break Tara's tower?" If you saw it happen, acknowledge the events that led to the offense. "I know you were upset that Tara used the best blocks, but . . ."

- Encourage accountability. Keep things simple with toddlers: "Tara is sad because you broke her tower." Begin to teach empathy to four- and five-year-olds: "I know you wanted to use the blocks, but you made Tara sad when you broke her tower." Older kids are capable of empathizing; link that to accountability by saying something like, "Tara worked hard on her tower. How did you make her feel when you broke it?"

- Encourage kids to own the problem and come up with a solution. Ask your school-age child, "What could you say or do to make her feel better?" and prompt your toddler, "We say *sorry* when we break things or make people sad."

- Model repentance and forgiveness. Say "I'm sorry" to your kids when you've spilled their milk or doodled on their work—and demonstrate forgiveness when they do the same things to you!

47. Is it OK to spank my child?

It wasn't until I became a parent that I realized how difficult it can be to stay cool in the face of a determined three-year-old. There were occasions where I lost it and used my hand when I should have used my brain. Fact is, you'll always win a battle when spanking is involved—you are twice the size and strength of the little person you are dealing with—but it will never be more than a short-term solution to a long-term problem. Seek out and use creative and loving alternatives instead.

It's also important here to recognize the difference between punishment and discipline. As *Kids Are Worth It!* author Barbara Coloroso points out, there is a huge difference:

> *Punishment is adult oriented, imposes power from without, arouses anger and resentment, invites more conflict, exacerbates wounds rather than heals them; is preoccupied with blame and pain; does not consider reasons or look for solutions; does something to a child; involves a strong element of judgment; and demonstrates a parent's ability to control a child.*
>
> *Discipline is not judgment, arbitrary, confusing, or coercive. It is not something that we do to children. It is working with them. It is a process that gives life to a child's learning. It is restorative and invites reconciliation. Its goal is to instruct, guide, and help children develop self-discipline—an ordering of the self from the inside, not an imposition from the outside.*

—Barbara Coloroso, from www.kidsareworthit.com, © 2009. Used by permission.

Research has overwhelmingly shown that spanking and other forms of physical punishment are harmful. Spanking teaches kids that hitting is OK. It emphasizes the negative behavior you want to stop, rather than

> A refusal to correct is a refusal to love: love your children by disciplining them.
>
> —Proverbs 13:24 *(The Message)*

encouraging the good behavior you want to promote. It's often done in anger—which can easily escalate into child abuse. And it takes away your child's dignity.

48. What should I do if I hear my child swear?

Kids have a knack for testing out swear words at the most inconvenient times. My nephew shared his word of choice while sitting beside his grandparents at our Christmas dinner. And I was speechless the day our four-year-old wandered into the kitchen and sweetly asked, "Mommy, what the **** are you doing?"

It's nearly impossible for kids to avoid hearing swear words and to resist the overwhelming desire to try them out. When your child does, here's what you can do:

- Stay calm. For most kids, trying out a swear word is like tasting a new flavor of bubblegum. They want to swirl it around in their mouth and then see what they can do with it. An overreaction from a parent makes it all the more exciting (and tempting!) to use.

- Talk about it. Explain what the word's meaning is and why your family doesn't say it. Also, encourage your child to let you know the next time she/he hears a new word or a word used in a way that sounds like it might be a swear word.

- Provide alternative words. For example, if the word your child used is one normally used in times of anger, talk about other non-offensive words that could be used instead.

- Follow through. If your child continues to use the offensive word, apply consequences such as a time out or loss of privileges.

- Lead by example. Make sure the words you use are pleasing to God and follow the same family rules and expectations.

49. How do I prepare my child to face peer pressure?

I clutched my keys and swallowed nervously as I stood with the other parents on the first day of kindergarten. As I watched my eager and smiling child get sucked through the school doors like an unsuspecting piece of Lego into a vacuum hose, my brain was swirling with questions: "What if the kids are mean?" "What if she doesn't make any friends?" "What if she *does* make friends and they tell her to jump off a bridge?"

My thoughts that day might have been irrational, but as parents we all worry about peer pressure. So how can we help our children stand up to peer pressure and make Jesus the leader they follow? Here are a few ideas.

- Build confidence. It takes confidence to say "No." Provide opportunities for your child to achieve success—whether that's as part of a team, by mastering a subject, or through a hobby. Remind your child that he is "fearfully and wonderfully made" by a perfect God (Ps. 139:14), and be sure that "I love you" is part of your daily conversations!

- Share your stories. Tell about times you gave in to peer pressure and wished you hadn't. Describe the times you stood up and did the right thing.

- Practice. Provide scenarios and practice possible responses. Ask, "What would you do if someone says they won't be your best friend if you're nice to another kid in your class?" or "What could you do if your friend wanted you to watch something you're not supposed to watch?" **Tip:** Write down some scenarios that you and your kids can pull from a hat and act out. Have your kids write down some situations too!

- Give direction. Teach your kids to follow THE leader—God. Memorize these words together: "Whatever you do, do it all for the glory of God (1 Cor. 10:32b, NIV) and encourage kids to use them as a decision-making guide.

50. My kids have unbelieving friends and friends of different faiths. Should I be worried about the influence those friends might have on my child's faith?

Judy Cook suggests, "Instead of beginning with a worry that 'the world' (unbelieving friends or friends of other faiths) might pull your children away from a relationship with God, try beginning with this thought: How wonderful that my children have an opportunity to be '*in* the world' with friends of different faiths or no faith in God, while I can help them to be 'not *of* the world.'"

Cook recommends that parents be very intentional about inviting their kids' friends—and their families as appropriate—into their homes. Let them see your faith in action through showing hospitality and loving acceptance to their friends as people who are loved by God. One of the wonderful things about having unbelieving friends and friends of other faiths is that it opens the door to conversations about faith with our kids as we share why we believe what we believe and as we talk to them about how to share their faith with others. As Cook points out, "Having to defend their beliefs will help your children become clearer about those beliefs."

51. What if my child picks friends I don't like?

I met Sam's friend Nigel at Sam's seventh birthday party. Nigel stuck his hand in the fishbowl, demanded a bigger piece of birthday cake at lunch, and rolled his eyes and said, "That's all we're getting?" after discovering the treat bags. I was deep-breathing and counting to ten in the kitchen when Sam burst in and said, "Isn't Nigel great, Mom?"

Our kids are going to choose their own friends, and we need to accept that they won't always choose the ones we would have picked. Here's what you can do when that happens:

- Show kindness. The "love your neighbor as yourself rule" applies to the Nigels in your child's life too.

- Avoid criticism. Telling your child that a friend is rude may make the friend seem more attractive, not less.

- Share your house rules. "Nigel, that's great balancing, but at our house we don't put the fine china on our heads."

- Check your assumptions. What is it that you don't like about the friend? Are you casting judgment based on stereotypes or other factors?

- Open your doors. Get to know your child's friends by inviting them to hang out at your house.

- Look at the positive. Your child will be choosing her own friends for the rest of her life; at some point she will have to stand up to peer pressure or face the consequences. These relationships may help your child develop some important critical thinking skills.

52. What about sleepovers when I don't know the family?

Your eight-year-old comes home from soccer practice thrilled because Bobby just invited him to a sleepover. You're thinking, "Bobby . . . isn't he the kid whose dad always yells at the referee? Isn't his mom the one who forgot to bring the snack last week? What if they yell at my child and forget to feed him?" Your child really wants to go and you're wondering if hiding a webcam in his pillow will make you feel less panic-stricken.

The solution: connect with the family before giving the OK to the sleepover. Call and find out what will be happening. Will they be watching movies? Playing videogames? Going online? A family whose home you'd feel safe sending your child to will have no problem with your questions—they'd want to know that same from you if you were hosting the event.

If you do allow the sleepover, discuss possible scenarios and responses in advance. For example, "My mom says I'm not allowed to go on the trampoline if there's more than one person on it" or "Can we play a different videogame? I'm not allowed to play that one." Understand that having the confidence to speak up at those times is not easy for most kids. Give them the "I'm not feeling well" option to save face if they'd rather come home. You'll also want to arrange for a call home at bedtime to say "Goodnight" and to ask your child, "Do you still want to sleep over?"

If you still don't feel comfortable, trust your instincts and say no. Explain to your child that you don't know the family well enough to allow a sleepover there. You might also offer to host the friend at your house instead.

53. How do I teach my kids to be respectful of others and also keep them safe from abuse?

Beth Swagman sums up the answer to this question in one word: *discernment.* It's what stands between being respectful to others and being assertive to prevent a wrong. To teach discernment to your child, Swagman suggests the following:

- In a non-frightening way, teach your child that *anyone* can harm a child. *Anyone* can include a relative, a teacher, a babysitter, someone they meet online, or someone at church. Help your child understand that nice people are capable of "bad touches" and that just because your child likes a person or a person is older than her or in charge of her, it doesn't mean she has to accept "bad touches."

- Teach your child the difference between a "good touch"—one that leaves a child happy and wearing a goofy grin—and a "bad touch"—one that leaves a child sad, feeling icky, and wanting to go home. Remind your child that anytime he or she gets a "bad touch" to tell you right away. (As a parent, remember that anyone who harms a child will try desperately to keep that child from telling a parent, so be alert when anyone gives gifts or money to your child for no apparent reason.)

- Explain to kids that some activities are not right. For example, there aren't any games where kids have to take their clothes off, and anyone who tells them they have to do that is lying. No one should take their picture or film them while undressed or in their underwear. Let your child know that a grownup should never ask a child not to tell his or her parents about something they did together. If any of these activities happen, tell your child to tell you right away.

- Know what your kids are doing online, and explain the dangers of meeting strangers in cyberspace. Tell kids never to give out personal information such as their full name, address, phone number, school name, or other identifying details. While you don't want to scare them, they need to know that the danger of online predators is a real one.

54. I suspect someone in our church has been abusive. Who do I tell?

"The first step will always be the hardest," says Beth Swagman. It's important not to deny what you see on your child's body or what your child describes to you—even though, like most parents, you'll want to seek some other explanation besides abuse for the injuries. You'll want to get angry or cry, but for your child's sake it's important to set your own feelings aside until you can confide in another adult.

The second step is to assess whether or not your child needs medical attention. Even though all injuries don't require medical attention, when they may be the result of abusive behavior a doctor's report could help investigators determine if abuse occurred. Again, put your reactions aside so that you can comfort your child—medical attention for an injury or assault can be a traumatic experience.

If the alleged incident took place in the past, or if there is no injury or sign of the alleged abuse, Swagman says your next step is to contact Children's Protective Services (United States), Children's Aid

Society (Canada), or the police. An official who has been trained to investigate reports of suspected abuse will come to your home and talk to your child there or, if the suspected abuser is a family member, the official will talk to your child at school or away from home.

Swagman acknowledges that it's not easy to call for help when you suspect child abuse, but your first priority—no matter how you are feeling—is to comfort and aid your child.

55. What do I do if I suspect my spouse or a friend or relative is abusing my child?

Seek outside help. And know that it's not un-Christian or unbiblical to get help when your child has been harmed by a family member.

Beth Swagman emphasizes that while we need to adopt a spirit of forgiveness for petty grievances and bigger grievances in order for marriages and other relationships to thrive, *the abuse of a child is neither petty nor a grievance issue.* In addition to the possibility that the behavior might be criminal, it's always a betrayal of trust, and that hurts a child at the core of his or her belief in self and in Jesus. Although we can still forgive the abuser, we must hold that person accountable. Swagman adds: "If you have a close relationship with an abuser, then it becomes harder to see the behavior as wrong and to seek help. While you struggle to believe the best about the abuser, the abuser will rationalize his or her bad behavior and try to convince you to ignore it. When someone you know has hurt your child, your pain as a parent and protector is so great that it is almost impossible for you to react. This means you must seek outside help.

56. Do Jesus' instructions in Matthew 18:15-17 mean I should deal with abusers (or suspected abusers) on my own or with church leadership instead of going to authorities?

No! Although there are times when it's appropriate for Christians to speak directly with someone whose conduct was unfair or unkind, situations of abuse and suspected abuse must be handled differently. In those situations you must go to civil authorities.

It's important to look beyond Jesus' instructions in Matthew 18:15-17 and examine his intent. Jesus' conflict resolution and problem-solving directives in Matthew 18 weren't intended for every situation and don't seem applicable when one person is abusing his or her authority over another or when the situation is a criminal matter.

Beth Swagman suggests looking back to Matthew 18:5-6, where Jesus says that an adult who harms a child will face very serious consequences. A conversation between the offender and the child (or the child's advocate) is not enough. She points out: "If a Christian may notify the police about a burglary, it seems unfathomable that Jesus would require a sit-down conversation with a child molester."

57. How do I prepare my child for change?

Starting school, moving away, getting a new sibling, making new friends, dealing with parental separation, becoming part of a blended family—life is full of transitions when you're a child. During those transitions it's important to give kids space to express their feelings. Ask if they have any questions, maintain their routines, and be positive. As a parent who loves the Lord you have another tool in your transition toolbox: trust in God. Here's how you can communicate that to your child in times of change:

- Talk to God. Pray together and let your child know that when you're apart you pray too! **Tip:** Write your prayers on a piece of paper or in a notebook and then watch for and record God's answers as a wonderful reminder that God is always listening.

- Hold on to God's promises. Learn a verse together and encourage your child to say those words when he or she needs some reassurance that God is taking care of things. (Proverbs 3:5-6, Psalm 56:3, and Philippians 4:13 are a few verses I've shared with my kids.) **Tip:** The words are easier to remember when you sing them!

- Share stories. Read Bible stories about God's work in the lives of people like Ruth (who moved far away), Joseph (who was separated from his family), Paul (who survived an earthquake), and Anna (who prayed and waited for a very long time). Read these stories not as examples of how to respond, but as reminders that God always has a plan. **Tip:** Share your own "God stories" too!

58. How can I encourage my child not to be materialistic?

It was a month before Christmas, and my kids were watching their favorite TV show while I enjoyed a coffee in the kitchen. Midway through the program I heard shouting and realized that as each new commercial came on, all four kids were pointing and shouting, "I want that! I want that!"

It's not easy to raise generous, non-materialistic kids when we're vying for their attention with product placements, clever commercials, and celebrity endorsements. But there are some ways to make your voice heard over all the "Buy me and be happy" messages:

- Lead by example. Are you demonstrating contentment or a desire for bigger and better? What does your child hear you say after leaving a friend's house? Do you talk about the amount of technology they own, the quality of the furniture, the size of the home? Are you embarrassed about your own lack of things?

- Treat your possessions as blessings from God and show you care more about people than stuff by sharing those gifts with others.

- Teach the difference between "wants" and "needs" and how that difference impacts what you buy.

- Say no. It's OK for your kids not to have everything they want. They will survive.

- Help your kids experience the pride of working and saving for something they really want.

- Encourage skepticism. Talk to your child about what she's viewing online and on TV and what's being offered for "free." Ask questions like "Why do you think that ad is being shown on this webpage during that show?" "Why do you think McDonald's gives out toys related to new movies?"

- Avoid treating a trip to the mall like a big adventure. (There's a reason malls feature food courts and amusement rides—the longer they keep you there, the more you're apt to buy.) Get what you need and then go.

- Share your worldview. Teach your child that the world belongs to God, not to people, and that God promises to provide for our needs. Explore Bible stories that show God's care for people and share personal stories of how God has provided for you!

59. How can I make it meaningful for my child to give financially to support God's work in the world?

Soon after Haiti was devastated by the 2010 earthquake, my church held a special Sunday-morning offering for the relief effort. Although the offering occurred after all the kids were dismissed for their children's ministry program, little Amy and Matthew stayed behind, each clutching a plastic sandwich bag filled with coins to pour into the offering plate. After hearing about the destruction in Haiti, Amy and Matthew had counted out pennies from their own savings so they could contribute. Their parents had a hunch that it was important for the kids to actually put their money into the offering plate. They were right!

Here's how you can make giving a meaningful experience for your child too:

- Make it real. Amy and Matthew saw images of Haiti on TV, knew there were children there who'd lost everything, and decided to help. Look for opportunities to make the cause or recipient real to your kids. Purchase canned food and deliver it to the food bank, shop for school supplies for a needy child in your community, "buy" a goat for a family in a developing country, and more.

- Make it personal. Rather than passing their kids a quarter to pop into the offering plate, Amy and Matthew's parents invited them to consider how much of their own money they could give, to gather it together, and to put it in the offering plate themselves. Other ways to make giving personal: offer your children earning opportunities to raise money for a cause they'd like to support at school; help set up a lemonade stand to raise money for a cause they care about; and if you give your child an allowance, encourage him or her to set aside a portion to give back to God. If you'd like your child to get into the habit of contributing to the offering at church, take the time on Saturday night to talk about who the recipient of the Sunday offering will be.

CHAPTER **4**

DAILY DETAILS, SPECIAL CELEBRATIONS

My kids are part of a French-immersion program at school, so for half of each day they are taught a variety of subjects in the French language. The theory behind this form of instruction is that immersing children in a language is much more effective than learning that language intermittently for a few hours each week. Of course, while my kids are able to speak French better than their non-immersion peers, extra instruction time won't make them completely fluent.

They'd need to live in a French-speaking community in order to *really* understand the language.

My people, hear my teaching;
listen to the words of my mouth.
I will open my mouth with a parable;
I will teach you lessons from the past—
things we have heard and known,
things our ancestors have told us.
We will not hide them from their descendants;
we will tell the next generation
the praiseworthy deeds of the LORD,
his power, and the wonders he has done.
He decreed statutes for Jacob
and established the law in Israel,
which he commanded our ancestors
to teach their children,
so the next generation would know them,
even the children yet to be born,
and they in turn would tell their children.
Then they would put their trust in God
and would not forget his deeds
but would keep his commands.

—Psalm 78:1-7

"Faith immersion" is no different. You can send your kids to church school; sign them up for girls' clubs and boys' clubs, and worship together in church every Sunday, but in order to *really* grow in faith, they need to move beyond learning about it—they need to *live* in it.

Faith is nurtured in the everyday rituals and activities—teachable moments, mealtime prayers, bedtime stories, and so on—and in special celebrations like Christmas, Easter, birthdays, faith milestones, and more. As the authors of *Children Matter* point out, ". . . children and adults are formed in the miniscule events of daily life, and those who have the most intimate relationships with children will influence their formation most profoundly, for good or ill. The home, then, is at the heart of spiritual formation for children and for their parents, and that formation takes place in the flow of everyday life" (p. 152).

How you "do" daily life with your children matters. It matters to God and it matters to your kids, whose experience of God is shaped by their experiences with you.

Questions

60. What are teachable moments and how can I best use them?

"Did you know that a python can swallow a goat whole?" "Did you know it's impossible to jump without bending your knees?" When kids share a fascinating fact it's because they experienced a "WOW" moment when they learned it. Educators know the value of those "WOW" experiences. They call them "teachable moments." They occur when a teacher seizes an unplanned opportunity to help a child make a connection or gain a new insight. As parents who know that faith nurture happens through ongoing conversations rather than one-time discussions, we can take advantage of teachable moments during daily life with our kids to instill in them a sense of "WOW" about God. Here are some ways to do that:

- Make connections as you wonder aloud together. Point out the sunlit sky at breakfast: "Look at the sky! How does God *do* that?" Mention the squirrels you see burying nuts in the park: "Isn't that cool how God wired squirrels' brains to get ready for winter? God thinks of everything!" Draw your child's attention to the variety of veggies at the supermarket: "Look at the colors and shapes and textures of the food in this row. God's imagination is incredible!"

- Introduce "WOW" moments into Bible reading by bringing in cool facts. Read David's words about the moon and stars in Psalm 8 and ask, "Did you know there's a shorter time between sunsets and moon-rises in the fall? In the days before tractor lights, it meant farmers had enough light to harvest their crops. God coordinated harvest with cooler, shorter days and more moonlight." After telling the story of creation, consider God's incredible imagination and wonderful design as you look up amazing facts about God's creatures together online or at the library.

- When your child experiences successes or failures, solves problems, worries about situations, starts something new, or sees something to completion, remind her that God is there, God is providing, God is loving, and God has a plan. And tell your child about the "teachable moments" when God spoke into your life too.

Finally, remember they're called "teachable moments," not "preach-able moments." Kids should get the connection through natural conversation, not a parental sermon!

61. How do we create family traditions and rituals?

On Sunday mornings when I was a girl, our family ate pastries for breakfast. Then, before heading to church, my brothers and I lined up for a pack of peppermints and a roll of salted licorice from our dad. While our Sunday-morning rituals weren't intended to prepare our hearts for worship, they were reminders that Sunday was special, and we connected them with going to church.

We've created traditions and rituals with our kids too: eating a "Beat the Winter Blues" dinner in our shorts in February, opening birthday gifts while being served breakfast in bed, taking a family photo in a pumpkin patch every Thanksgiving, and never leaving the house without saying, "Bye, I love you!" These repeated events make memories and draw us closer together as a family.

Family traditions and rituals can also provide ways to help our kids connect with God and to remind ourselves of God's faithfulness. Some—like adding Jesus to the nativity scene on Christmas Day, lighting a candle on baptism anniversaries, joining hands in prayer around the table on Easter—will be connected to specific Christian celebrations. Others, like praying before a meal, playing music that glorifies God as you prepare for church, or reading a Bible story at bedtime, flow naturally out of the simple patterns of everyday life.

The best way to create these special times is to look for ways to include God in both in the special celebrations and the daily details of your family's life. Before you know it, you've begun a tradition—and your kids will be the first to complain if you try to change it!

62. How do we read the Bible together?

When I was a kid, most families I knew read a denominational devotional booklet for suppertime devotions. The Bible passage was read first, then the daily devotional, then, finally, the prayer at the bottom of the page was muttered in monotone before everyone fled from the table.

In many cases, we *heard* the Bible reading, but we never really *listened*. While the content of those devotions was probably great, what was missing was enthusiasm—the kind you show when you're about to sink your fork into a fabulous piece of pie or head outdoors on an exciting adventure.

When you read the Bible with children, you want them to do more than *hear* what you're reading—you want them to listen in a way that helps them see the connections between the Bible stories, their personal stories, and God. That means reading the Bible as a book of discovery every time you open it.

When her children were babies, Karen-Marie Yust would read the Bible animatedly and out loud "so they would know that the Bible is filled with stories worth hearing." She offers the following practical suggestions to help make reading the Bible with your kids meaningful:

- Toddlers and preschoolers: Choose passages that have repetitious phrases (the creation story and the psalms are good examples) and invite your child to echo the repeated words so they'll become familiar with the vocabulary of the Bible and the people in it. Read and tell stories with an expressive voice, showing your excitement about God's story.

- School-age children: Challenge each other to consider how stories in the Bible are similar to and different from your own lives. Wonder about the details that aren't in the text, and think about how the perspective offered in the story might connect to something today. For example, what might the stories of King Solomon's wisdom tell us about how to use the Internet wisely? How do the stories of Jesus' friendship with tax collectors and other "undesirable" people suggest we should treat homeless people?

63. How do I get kids interested in Bible stories?

The Bible—God's love story to the world—is filled with mystery and mayhem, murder and romance, solutions, surprises, and more. But often when we pull it out of the drawer to read it, our kids roll their eyes in boredom.

In his book *Helping Our Children Grow in Faith,* author Robert J. Keeley talks about the importance of sharing stories in a way that encourages kids to *live into them.* Keeley does this by asking "wondering questions" about the story and inviting listeners to think about how the people felt and why they did the things they did. For example, after reading the Esther story, Keeley wonders how Esther felt when she first arrived at the palace. He's also curious about whether Esther planned to have two banquets all along, or if she chickened out at the first one and so had to quickly organize a second.

Asking questions like these—with no right or wrong answers—gets kids interested in Bible stories because they invite kids to *actively* listen and respond.

It's also important to remember that the people in the Bible were living, breathing, moving people just like you and me. Changing your voice and adding facial expressions when you tell their stories will make "Bible people" come alive for your kids. So will finding their locations on a map, a globe, or in an online search.

Finally, consider changing locations to go with the story—sit outside to read the story of creation, crawl under the table to read a psalm about how God surrounds and protects us. Or connect stories to your meal—try fish for supper and talk about what it means to be "fishers of people" during dessert!

64. How do I encourage my child to spend time with God each day?

Have you ever seen a three-year-old talk on a cell phone? He nods while murmuring words of agreement, asks questions, and holds the phone like adults do. Children love to copy and imitate the behaviors of others around them. And, just as you model vocabulary, actions, and even how to talk on a phone, you're also modeling how to spend time with God each day. Karen-Marie Yust says, "If we want children to spend daily time with God, they need to see us doing so. Even better, they need to spend time with God alongside us so that they experience the support and encouragement of our company."

Share devotional time with your children. Cradle your infant in your arms as you sing praises or read Scripture. Cuddle your preschooler as you read a bedtime Bible story and talk to God together. Share quiet times with God as you both close your eyes, breathe in deeply, then pause to listen and pray. Encourage your school-age child to settle in before prayer (Yust suggests singing a song like "Be Still and Know" or saying the words of a Taizé chorus to help prepare) and to pause for reflection after reading the Bible.

Tip: Wondering aloud together about what you've read is a great way to encourage reflection.

A friend once shared how every night he would see his dad kneel beside his bed to pray and what a deep impression that left on him. Let your kids "catch" you spending time with God on your own—outside of family devotional time—and tell them about the things you've been reading in the Bible and talking about with God.

65. How do I know which Bible translation or Bible storybook is best to use with my kids?

My eleven-year-old daughter, Tara, attends a club at her friend's church. When I expressed my surprise that they were using the King James version of the Bible in their study group, Tara said, "Well, that *is* the real Bible, Mom. It's the *Holy* Bible." With the variety of different covers on the Bibles in our home and at church, Tara had never actually seen a Bible that simply identified itself as a Holy Bible before!

It can be overwhelming to choose a family Bible from the vast number of choices in translations (and covers!) that are available. With my school-age kids we've been reading *The Message*—a contemporary language paraphrase of the Bible—and using the New Revised Standard Version (NRSV) and Today's New International Version (TNIV) translations to check different interpretations of what we're reading. Leonard Vander Zee recommends using the Contemporary English Version (CEV) or the New International Readers Version (NIrV) for kids younger than grade 5, and challenging older kids with your favorite "adult" version.

When it comes to Bible storybooks, look for those with illustrations that portray God's people as the vibrant, diverse people they were, rather than as cartoons or all-white characters. Avoid Bibles that tack a moral onto the end of the story, and look for those that emphasize *God's* story, not the heroics of a character. And, as Yust points out, help kids understand the difference between "stories about Bible stories" and the Bible itself, so they don't become confused about why their Bibles are so different from an "adult Bible."

Great Bible storybooks and picture books

- *At Break of Day* by Nikki Grimes
- *God Loves Me* storybooks by Pat Nederveld
- *The Jesus Storybook Bible* by Sally Lloyd-Jones
- *Spark* story Bible from Augsburg Fortress
- *Tomie dePaola's Book of Bible Stories* by Tomie dePaola
- *The Lord's Prayer* and *Psalm 23* by Tim Ladwig
- *The Baby Bible* by Sarah Toulmin
- *Psalm 23* by Barry Moser
- *The Light of the World* by Katherine Paterson
- *The Ten Commandments for Children* by Lois Rock
- *The Easter Story* by Brian Wildsmith
- *The Children of God Storybook* by Desmond Tutu

—Jane Schuyler, Resource Specialist for the Reformed Church in America

66. How do I teach my child to pray?

I don't remember the required reading, the final exam, or the other students in my favorite university course at Dordt College in Sioux Center, Iowa. What I do remember and what I looked forward to most each day was Dr. Westra's opening prayer. He'd look at us all with this big smile on his face, say "Let's talk to God," and then start praying a prayer like this:

Hi, God.

> *What an awesome day you made today. The raindrops fed all the flowers, and the puddles are perfect for jumping in. Thanks for shady trees and yo-yo strings. Thanks for giving us elbows so we can bend our arms in so many ways. How do you think of such cool things, Lord? Please watch over our friends who aren't here today: the ones with runny noses, the ones who are feeling sad, and those who are far away. And, God, we're sorry for hurting people's feelings and not doing the stuff we're supposed to do. Thanks for loving us even when we mess up.*

> *We love you, Lord. Amen.*

My professor modeled his belief that prayer is a real conversation with God—a time when you can share what's on your heart, seek God's blessing, say you're sorry, and ask for help. The best way to teach your child to pray is by including your child in your conversations with God as you pray in front of and with your child. And because there are a variety of ways to communicate with God in prayer, consider doing some of the following together as well:

- Memorize a prayer. Learn a specific prayer you can say together at bedtime or mealtime or during another part of your daily routine. **Tip:** When you use a memorized prayer, including a time to pause and pray in your own words together helps your child remember that she isn't reciting a poem, but communicating with God.

- "Be still and know" God together. Karen-Marie Yust encourages parents and children to spend time together in silent prayer and listen for God's voice or feel God's presence. **Tip:** Giving younger children a ball of clay to squeeze may help relax them, while older kids may find it easier to let go of thoughts as they concentrate on a lit candle or a simple image or by repeating a word or phrase as they breathe slowly.

- Engage their bodies. Yust suggests encouraging children to use their whole body in prayer by raising their hands in praise and thanksgiving, getting down on their knees or lying down to show they are sorry as they ask for forgiveness, holding their hands open on their laps when asking God to provide for them, and holding up their hands as a sign of blessing when asking God to take care of and bless the world.

67. How do I encourage my child to pray?

When our daughter Kailey was five, she used prayer as ammunition, opening one eye and squinting across the dinner table at her older sister while pointedly praying, "And, Lord, please make Sam stop sucking her thumb." Now a teenager, Kailey regularly leads our family in heartfelt, honest conversations with God. Our eyes have welled up more than once as she prayed for something that we would have struggled to verbalize. Unlike Kailey, I didn't feel comfortable praying out loud until I was an adult—and even now I'm more at ease praying with a group of kids than I am with my peers. Whether you're a Kailey or a Karen when it comes to prayer, it's important that you encourage your child to have regular conversations with God. Here's how:

Pray regularly. Having set times for prayer, such as before a meal or at bedtime, is important because it makes prayer a daily habit.

Pray anytime and anywhere. Prayer should be as natural and necessary as breathing! Talk to God together on the way to school, pause to pray when you pass an accident, and tell God you love what he's done with the trees as you stroll through the woods.

Pray from the heart. To show that prayer is a conversation, feel free to use your own words when you talk with God. **Tip:** Avoid the temptation to praise a child's prayer or to laugh while they are praying. When kids have to consider the reactions of others to their prayers, they can become self-conscious.

Pray for each other. Let your child know you are praying for her when she's at school, away from home, or having a difficult time. Ask your child to pray for you too! **Tip:** Pray silently or out loud for the person to your right during meal times.

Prayers to try at home

- **A.C.T.S. prayer:** Teach your child the four parts of prayer (adoration, confession, thanksgiving, supplication) by replacing the initials with these kid-friendly categories: "I love you, God" "I'm sorry," "thank you," and "please"—and use those topics to guide your prayers.
- **Echo prayer:** One person prays one line at a time and the other person repeats it.
- **Written prayer:** Beginning with the Lord's Prayer, discover some beautiful age-appropriate prayers that you can learn together with your child. Written or set prayers will sometimes get you and your child through difficult times when spontaneous prayer is difficult. (For starters you can find the "Serenity Prayer" or the "Prayer of Saint Francis" on the Web.)
- **Circle prayer:** One person starts and the next person adds a sentence. **Tip:** Hold hands while you do this.
- **Popcorn prayers:** After one person begins the prayer, other can jump in and add a prayer as they feel led to do so. **Tip:** Choose a

specific prayer topic, such as thanking God or looking forward to the first day of school.

- **Sung prayer:** Sing or listen to a song of praise together. **Tip:** Make up a prayer to the tune of a familiar song.
- **Journal prayer:** Write down specific prayer requests in a journal, or keep a list on the fridge. Look back regularly to see how God has answered those prayers.
- **Motion prayer:** Use your body or hands to create movement and sign language along with the words you're praying. **Tip:** This form of prayer works especially well with children who are nonverbal or have difficulty communicating. (Visit www.friendship. org to purchase *Learning the Lord's Prayer,* a kinesthetic version of the Lord's Prayer.)
- **Silent prayer:** Be still and know God (Ps. 46:10). Light a candle or play music before pausing quietly together in silence with God. In her book *Real Kids, Real Faith,* Karen-Marie Yust suggests starting with a repeated word or phrase such as "shalom" or "Jesus loves me, this I know." **Tip:** Repeat that word or phrase again if you become distracted.

68. How can I make God part of our bedtime routine?

Bedtime routines can be time-consuming, but giving kids your undivided attention for five to fifteen minutes each night offers you an incredible opportunity to connect with each other and with God. Here's how:

Cuddle up and connect. Talk to your preschooler about his day and share your pride at his accomplishments. Share some awe and wonder about the way God made his body to move and created perfect puddles to jump in. Ask your school-aged child, "What made you laugh today?" "What was the best part of your day?" "What was the hardest part of your day?" "Where did you see God today?"

Listen to music. Play music that glorifies God as you dance with your preschooler to get those last wiggles out. With your school-age child, sing along with a worship song or just lie down and listen to it together. Play music in the background as you talk, read, and pray.

Read together. Grab a children's story Bible or devotional book and read it together. Early readers will be proud to read a page to you; older kids will love the shared experience of diving into a book each night.

Talk to God out loud together. Keep it simple: "Hi, God. Before Sam goes to sleep we want to talk to you for a while." Get your child involved by asking if he or she would like to start or end the prayer. Try the occasional popcorn prayer in which you start the prayer and then either one of you can jump in with a sentence to God. Focus younger kids by having a popcorn prayer to thank God or to ask for forgiveness, and so on.

69. How do we make celebrations part of our faith walk?

Birthdays, graduations, and anniversaries are a big deal in the Dutch-Canadian culture in which I was raised. When I was a child and my grandparents would come over to celebrate my birthday, they wouldn't just congratulate me—they'd also congratulate my parents, my siblings, and other relatives, saying, "Congratulations on your daughter's (or sister's or niece's or granddaughter's) birthday!" They did the same thing for graduations, anniversaries, baptisms, and anything else we were celebrating.

Two other things I could count on were receiving a card with a handwritten Bible verse or a note about God's work in my life, and one of my grandparents pausing during the celebration to look around the room and say, "What a blessing!"

What I didn't appreciate then, and what I know now, is that they were taking the opportunity to teach me to acknowledge God's gifts and to draw me closer to God on those special occasions that I might have thought were "all about me." As parents we can follow the lead of my grandparents and take time on the special days in the life of our child and our family to thank and praise God for his faithfulness.

70. How do we keep our Christmas celebrations focused on God?

The first year I hung a Jesse Tree Advent calendar on the wall, I envisioned four cherub-faced children and one thoughtful husband carefully listening to me read the devotionals each night before solemnly hanging an ornament on the tree.

In reality, for twenty-five days four cranky kids and their frustrated dad wiggled and complained as I read, then fought over whose turn it was to hang the ornament.

In spite of that disastrous first year, the hanging of the Jesse Tree is now a DeBoer family Christmas tradition (thanks to some attention-span adjustments I made to the devotionals and the creation of an elaborate turn-taking plan for hanging the ornaments).

The first way to focus your Christmas celebrations on what is important is to remember that perfection doesn't exist on earth. It's less important that everything goes off without a hitch than it is that meaningful traditions are built. The second is to be intentional about surrounding your kids with more of the biblical Christmas than the commercial one. Here are some ideas to help you do that:

- If your child believes in Santa Claus and you're OK with that, try celebrating his arrival (or the gift giving) on a different day from your celebration of Jesus' birth. When our kids were little some gifts came from Santa and some came from us, but they all arrived under the tree the morning *before* Christmas Day. Once the gift giving and receiving was done, we were able to focus our kids' attention on Jesus' birthday.

- Light Advent candles—adding one each Sunday night—for the four weeks leading up to Christmas. Light a fifth candle on Christmas Day.

- Include ornaments on your tree that symbolize parts of the Christmas story, and talk about them while you decorate: "What do the stars remind you of?" "Which part of the Christmas story do the angels make you think about?"

- Sing, listen to, and play Christmas carols and songs about Jesus' birth.

- Set up a nativity set that your child can touch and use to act out the Christmas story. **Tip:** Some families wait until Christmas Day to add the baby Jesus figure, wrapping it up as a gift for the kids to open and place in the manger.

- Attend church services and family Christmas concerts together.

- Visit outdoor live nativity scenes in your city.

- Light candles on a cake and sing "Happy Birthday" to Jesus.

- Purchase or check the library for picture books about the birth of Jesus. Stand picture books up on a table as part of your Christmas display.

- Create anticipation for Jesus' birth by using a Jesse Tree to count down the days to Christmas. The tree can be a small Christmas tree or a branch brought in from outdoors. Search "Jesse Tree" at www.rca.org for free Jesse Tree devotionals and ornament patterns.

- Keep gifts simple. The best gifts we ever exchanged as a family weren't the most expensive—they weren't even on anyone's list. They were the result of exchanging names with the kids and giving each one $5.00 to spend. The only rule was that the gift had to come from a thrift store that helped others in the community or that supported a worthy cause.

- Give back as a family in a way that's meaningful for your kids. Fill a box together for an organization such as Operation Christmas Child, go shopping for groceries to donate to the Food Bank, buy hats and mittens for homeless people, or let your child choose a gift (goats, school supplies, mosquito nets, and so on) that you can purchase online as a donation to a denominational ministry.

- Demonstrate joy. Let your child see the joy that Jesus' birth brings you, even when circumstances are difficult.

71. How do we keep our Easter celebrations focused on God?

Each December I haul boxes of Christmas decorations out of the basement, turn the buffet table into a nativity scene, and coat the house with cranberry-colored wreaths, bright lights, and bows. One Christmas as I stood in the kitchen sprinkling silver balls on sugar cookies, seven-year-old Kailey wandered in and asked, "Mom, how come you decorate the whole house for Christmas but you don't do anything special for Easter? Isn't Easter just as important as Christmas?" (Don't you hate it when your kids are wiser than you are?)

Easter *should* be anticipated and celebrated with the same awe and wonder as Christmas. Here are some ways to share the significance of Easter with your family:

- Read and reflect. You might start with the Palm Sunday story on Palm Sunday and continue with a reading each day through Easter Monday. Wonder together about the sounds and sights in the story, why things happened as they did, and how Jesus, his friends, the soldiers, and others might have felt. Share how the story makes you feel too! **Tip:** Give each person a notepad in which to write or draw impressions of the stories you've read each day.

- If your church has Holy Week services or liturgies (Maundy Thursday, Good Friday, Easter Vigil), take the kids along, and talk to them about the special meaning of these gatherings.

- Make a set of Resurrection Eggs—an egg carton with twelve plastic eggs containing symbols of the Easter story—and use them to tell and retell the story together. **Tip:** Do an online search of "resurrection eggs" for symbol ideas.

- Purchase palm fronds to wave on Palm Sunday and use them as a table decoration for the rest of the week.

- Create Easter cards together and send them to family and friends.

- Check out picture books on the true meaning of Easter from your local library or church library. Decorate your home by putting the books on display. **Tip:** *Benjamin's Box* by Melody Carlson is a wonderful picture book with ideas for Resurrection Eggs.

- Make a mural that shows Jesus' journey from Jerusalem to heaven. Invite your child to add a picture each day as you share more of the story.

- Hang up balloons and streamers while your child is sleeping on the night before Easter so she'll wake up to a sunrise surprise.

72. What are faith milestones and why should we celebrate them?

In the religious culture in which I grew up, several milestones were observed and celebrated: baptism, Sunday school graduation, and public profession of faith. North American culture recognizes other milestones, including taking your first steps, losing your first tooth, starting school, graduating from school, getting your driver's license, getting your first cell phone, getting your first job, and retirement.

As Christ-followers we know that God is a part of *all* these significant moments in our lives. A faith milestone can be defined as "a marker along life's journey that says, 'This is something important and God is here, too.' It is time to pause, to celebrate, to share the joys and sorrows, to give and receive support, to reflect on where and how we have found God in our story" (Marilyn Sharpe, March 2005 "Faith Milestones," www.youthandfamily institute.org). Celebrating faith milestones with your family is a wonderful way to remind kids that God is faithful and present in all the details of their lives.

73. What are some milestones we can celebrate as a family?

After God told the Israelites to take twelve stones from the Jordan River and make them into a memorial, he said to the Israelites,

*In the future when your descendants ask their parents, "What do these stones mean?" tell them, "Israel crossed the Jordan on dry ground." For the L*ORD *your God dried up the Jordan before you until you had crossed over. The L*ORD *your God did to the Jordan what he had done to the Red Sea when he dried it up before us until we had crossed over. He did this so that all the peoples of the earth might know that the hand of the L*ORD *is powerful and so that you might always fear the L*ORD *your God.*

—Joshua 4:21-24

Below you'll find a list of some possible milestones to celebrate with your child—and space to add your own ideas.

- baptism
- profession of faith/confirmation

- graduation from nursery to children's worship/ Sunday school
- graduation from children's worship/Sunday school
- first day of school
- first communion
- losing your first tooth (celebrating the fact that your child is growing older)
- learning to ride a bike (celebrating growing independence)
- birthdays
- receiving a driver's license
- voting in an election for the first time
- graduation from school
- starting a new job
- moving
-
-
-

Faith Milestone Resources

Celebrating the Milestones of Faith by Laura Keeley and Robert J. Keeley

www.youthandfamilyinstitute.org

74. How do I do family devotions when I have kids of different ages?

Doing devotions with kids of different ages can be challenging, but it's important to spend time with God together as a family. Follow these ideas to make the most of your time together:

Set a signal. Indicate that this time is special by lighting a candle or singing a song or opening with a call ("Now it's time . . . ") and response ("to hear God's story!").

Keep things simple. Save the longer readings with your older kids for one-on-one times or give your wee ones a Bible storybook to hold or some play dough to mold while you finish up with the older kids. **Tip:** Pass a ball of play dough to your preschooler and invite him to shape something from the story.

Invite participation. Have kids act out the Bible story while you read it a second time. Select a child to act as a blob of "clay" that you (or his sibling) can "sculpt" to show the main characters' actions as you tell the story. Invite your kids to read the characters' lines using interesting voices. (It's OK to laugh when you do devotions!) Pause while reading the story to wonder about the details that aren't there. Encourage younger kids to draw pictures of what is being read and share the picture afterwards.

75. When can we do devotions if we don't eat together?

Between work, school, carpools, and other commitments, finding time to eat and do devotions together can seem like an impossible task. The great news is that God is with you wherever you go. Family devotions don't have to be restricted to the dinner table, so you can have them in all the other places you gather together: in bedrooms, outdoors, in the car, and on the playroom floor.

A rainy-day fort is a great place to read a Bible story or psalm together. The drive home from soccer practice is a wonderful time to belt out a song of praise. A walk to the store is a perfect time to point out God's awesome creation and say a prayer of thanksgiving. Be aware of the teachable moments God provides you every day and use them for an impromptu devotion.

Although family time may be limited during the week, you can make the most of the moments you do have together by turning off technology, letting voicemail take calls, and having your inbox hold texts.

Show kids that the time you spend together learning about God is important.

76. How do we make time for God on family vacations?

Ahh, the family road trip. Fights over the window seat, complaints about how long it's taking, constant reminders that somebody has to pee—and that's just the first hour! The bad news about driving together is that you're all buckled in the same 5'x7' area for an extended period of time. Of course, that's also the good news—you have each other's undivided attention for the duration of the trip!

Resist the temptation to "take a break" from God when you're on vacation. It's probably one of the best times to nurture faith because your family is relaxed and has all the time in the world to reflect and wonder together. Here's how to make the most of that time:

- Make music. While the silence that a van full of iPods provides may be priceless, don't miss the opportunity to listen—and sing!—together. Set aside some time to listen to music that glorifies God. Give everyone the opportunity to request both a silly song and a song from church that you can belt out together.

- Point out the "God-prints." My husband is big on clouds and trees and sunsets. He points them out to the kids, saying, "How does God *do* that? It's *amazing!*" Sometimes the kids respond, sometimes they just roll their eyes, but that's OK—we're training them to be future God-print seekers too!

- Bring a story Bible. Pack a story Bible and let your child pick favorite stories to read (David and Goliath five nights in a row is OK!).

- Develop devotionals. Get a dollar-store notebook. Set aside a page for each day and add a "God Connection," such as, "Things I saw today that reminded me of God," "Thank you, God, for . . .", "I'm so glad God gave us . . .", and so on. Look at that day's heading in the morning and set aside time at the end of the day to add pictures or words to the page. **Tip:** Insert completed devotional pages into a photo album of your trip so those connections become part of family history.

77. What does it mean to celebrate Sabbath together? How do we do that?

God knows that doing life at a hundred miles an hour 24/7 is a bad idea. In fact, God gave us a great example to follow from the very beginning: God rested, enjoyed the fruits of his labor, and declared it a Holy Day. It's important to regularly press "pause" on the treadmill that school, sports, and even church commitments can keep our families on. Sabbath is really all about freedom—freedom from our work and responsibilities, and freedom to enjoy God and his creation. Being intentional about using that pause button to spend uninterrupted time in relationship with God and your family is what it means to celebrate Sabbath.

Probably the hardest thing about celebrating Sabbath is marking the date/time on your calendar. Once you've made that commitment, here are some things you can do:

- Turn off technology—phones, Internet, and so on—for a few hours (or for a full day if you can handle it!).

- Enjoy a special snack or meal reserved just for your Sabbath celebration.

- A Jewish Sabbath begins with a festive candlelit meal at sunset on Friday evening. Think about doing the same on Saturday, or just light a candle and place it in the center of your dinner table as a reminder that God is there.

- Take a moment at the end of a meal or during your family time together to "be still and know God" with a moment of silence. Help younger kids focus by giving them something to reflect on, such as things they're thankful for.

- Skip the mall, avoid the grocery store, set aside your errand list.

- End a family meal with a popcorn prayer of praise to God (see p. 120).

- Enjoy creation together. Go for a walk, play soccer, pick apples, build a snowman, or gather leaves and other bits of nature to glue on a creation collage when you get home.

- Make something together. Paint a picture, bake bread, play with play dough, write a song or poem, decorate cookies.

- Relax and read in the same room together.

- Visit a museum; thank God together for color, texture, and light.

- Play a board game.

- Listen to music that glorifies God, sing a favorite song together, or search online for music videos that you can watch as you sing along.

- Flip through a photo album and share stories of God's faithfulness to your family.

CHAPTER **5**

CHALLENGES AND TRANSITIONS

On the days when my family life is in complete chaos, I take great comfort knowing that the families in the Bible also lived troubled lives. Cain killed his brother, Abraham pretended his wife was his sister, Noah's kids found him naked and drunk, and Rebekah tricked her husband to help her favorite son! The amazing thing is that not only did God never give up on his children, God kept the covenant promises and continued to bless them! Genesis 28 tells how Jacob (who, by the way, lied to his father and favored his son) heard God's voice present a powerful promise:

> *He had a dream in which he saw a stairway resting on the earth, with its top reaching to heaven, and the angels of God were ascending and descending on it. There above it stood the LORD, and he said: "I am the LORD, the God of your father Abraham and the God of Isaac. I will give you and your descendants the land on which you are lying. Your descendants will be like the dust of the earth, and you will spread out to the west and to the east, to the north and to the south. All peoples on earth will be blessed through you and your offspring. I am with you and will watch over you wherever you go, and I will bring you back to this land. I will not leave you until I have done what I have promised you" (Gen. 28: 12-15).*

As part of God's family through Jesus, we know that God also promises to bless us, be with us, watch over us, and never leave us. Now that's something to hold on to when you're facing family challenges and transitions!

But the story gets even better. Jacob wakes up from that incredible dream and says, "Surely the LORD is in this place, and I was not aware of it" (Gen. 28:16). Jacob, son of Isaac, future father of Israel, and soon-to-be wrestler with God, was unaware of God's presence. I wonder how often I've also been unaware.

On those days when you feel overwhelmed, confused, disappointed, hurt, uncertain, and anxious, be aware that God is there. God—whom Paul calls "the Father of mercies and the God of all consolation" (2 Cor. 1:3b, NRSV) is with you every step of the way, just as God was with your rebellious relatives in the stories of Genesis.

Questions

78. How do I explain death to my child?

When my five-year-old daughter found her fish named Frieda floating belly-up in her tank, I told her that Frieda was swimming the backstroke and suggested we leave the room to give Frieda some privacy. Then I raced to the phone and frantically begged my husband to pick up a matching fish that we could quietly exchange for the deceased. Ron wisely declined, and I did as he suggested: I shared the sad news with our daughter and then held a funeral on our front lawn. Since then, our children have experienced the death of a friend, the loss of a friend's parent, and the passing away of family members. While finding "the right words" is never easy, Jan Talen offers the following practical advice:

- Be factual (but not overly descriptive) and calm when sharing information with your child, especially when dealing with a young child who thinks in very literal and concrete terms and may misinterpret the euphemisms we sometimes use for death. Talen encourages parents to be specific and to use physical terms: "Grandma's heart stopped working and she isn't breathing anymore." Then invite your child to say back to you what she heard and understood. To get a sense of how much your child understands and to know how to continue the conversation, you might ask her what she thinks death means and what it means to her that this person has died.

- Invite your child to talk about (and to continue talking about) his feelings as well as the changes that the death may bring (or has already brought) to his life. (Young children may not be able to grasp the permanent nature of death when it occurs, but might have struggles and questions as time passes.) Keep in mind that children will respond in very different ways. Some will wonder why we can't make the person breathe again. Others might understand that the person is dead but won't know what to do with the emotions they are experiencing. Some will feel powerless because they couldn't fix things, or confused that their parents couldn't make everything better. Others might worry about the safety of their world and whether they or another loved one will die soon too. Affirm their sadness, confusion, and anger. Address any sense of powerlessness with assurances that the world as they know it is safe (and if it wasn't safe, share how the adults in their life have made it safe now). Talen also suggests that it helps to acknowledge the good things the person who died brought into your life when they were living and to find ways to still enjoy some of those good things. For example, Mom loved to play piano, so listening to piano music might be a good way to remember and enjoy some of Mom after she's gone.

- Explain that a very special part of the person is now living safe and whole with Jesus and that Jesus loves that person and is taking care of him or her. Even though we are sad because we miss the person who died, he or she isn't hurting or sad anymore. Remind your child that when Jesus comes back people who believe in him will be able to live with him forever.

Some basics for helping children through any difficult circumstance:

- Affirm and enjoy them and their daily lives.
- Keep them well fed and on a basic schedule, with options for play and creativity (not too much screen time) and a regular place to sleep with a regular bedtime.
- Hold their hands, touch them, hug them, and look them in the eyes. Children often feel shame and guilt for the circumstances that the adults are in; kind, truthful eye contact and affirmation of the child's positive character attributes are crucial.
- Give them the information they want to know. In other words, let the child ask the questions about the situation, and answer what they ask without adding more information.
- Keep your own emotions and thoughts about blame or responsibility mostly to yourself. Kids will look to you for clues about how awful their world is. If you are poorly behaved or emotionally wild, they will follow you with the belief that they made your world bad.
- Keep adult information to adults; do not share it with children. They do not need to know the specifics of an affair, an intense marriage dis-

agreement, or gruesome details of a person's death.

- Children can absorb and assimilate about as many sentences as their age. Almost always, one of those sentences needs to be affirming, reassuring the child that he is safe and fine because you will be safe and fine too.
- A child's faith is straightforward. Encourage kids to pray and to trust in Jesus for their own hurt and fright. Do not promise that Jesus will make everything and everyone OK again. You *can* promise with certainty that Jesus is always with us and caring about us, even when things are not OK.
- Relate to your child and build a relationship; do not just demand respect. Remember that rules without reason create rebellion.
- Consistent, clear, and calm attitudes and behavior create confidence in children. Cruelty and crabbiness kills confidence.
- Get professional support and advice if you can not maintain your own emotional stability or your child is struggling to maintain his or her emotional balance.
- Pray for your child daily and specifically.

—Jan Talen

79. How do I explain the mental illness of a family member to my kids?

Children like their world to be predictable and understandable. Mental illness can be disruptive and mysterious, leading kids to feel confused, anxious, and embarrassed. Jan Talen says it's important to use gentle honesty and truth when explaining mental illness. She suggests that you define mental illness to your child by saying, "The person's brain is not working just right, and that can make the person sad or tired or angry."

Tell your child that the person with the mental illness doesn't *want* to have it—just like your child doesn't want to have a cold or the flu—and that the person is doing what he or she can to get well, though sometimes that might take a long time.

Reassure your child—often if necessary—that she didn't break or hurt the person's brain and that she can't fix it; that's the job of the doctors and the person with the illness. As your child grows up, you'll be able to share more facts about the illness, equipping her to respond to and deal with it in healthy ways.

Talen also points out that sometimes a person with a mental illness may find it difficult to show love or to be kind or happy. Let your child know that this doesn't mean he or she doesn't love the child, just that the person's brain won't let him or her show it right now. To help your child understand the illness and minimize any guilt she might experience about feeling embarrassed or responsible, it's important that you regularly encourage your child to talk about her experiences or fears and give her the freedom and opportunity to ask questions.

80. How do I help my child deal with my divorce?

First, it's very important that you and your spouse sit down with your child together and share the news in an age-appropriate way—reassuring your child both of your continued love for him and that you are divorcing each other, not him. Be prepared for your child to feel very unsettled as you move through the process of separation and divorce. As Jan Talen points out, your child's life has been built on a foundation of trust and truth between two adults, and when that base breaks, children feel those effects deeply. She suggests the following two "keeps" to help steady that base through tough times:

1. Keep your own spiritual, behavioral, and emotional life as stable as possible. Children follow their parents'

lead, so when a parent is deeply struggling in these areas the children are likely to struggle as well.

2. Set and keep clear and consistent boundaries with your spouse and your child. Some specific suggestions include

- Keep your divorce conversations and arguments away from your child, as he will have a natural inclination to feel responsible and want to fix it.

- Be consistent and dependable with family behavioral rules to help give your child a sense of control and safety in a world that may feel very unstable or chaotic.

- Deal with the details to help your child cope with his uncertainty. Write down schedules with specifics about school projects and activities, regular homework, sports, holidays, visitations, birthdays, and so on, so that Mom, Dad, and child all have the same calendar. Maintain trust by following the schedule and communicating changes.

- Answer your child's questions about these life-changing choices factually and empathically, without blame or accusation. Be aware of your parental and marriage boundaries. Kids do not need to know everything; they mostly want to know if you are in control when things aren't going right.

- Affirm, enjoy, and encourage. Speak to the positive side of circumstances. Criticize less and listen more. Parent intentionally and calmly.

- Be aware that in the circumstances of divorce, you may be too overwhelmed yourself to always deal sensitively and honestly with your child's struggles. If you see signs that your child is settling into unhealthy feelings or behaviors, don't hesitate to seek counseling for or with him. Some schools, churches, and other organizations also offer groups for kids of divorcing parents.

- Assure your child that Jesus never leaves. Your child might think that if a parent can leave her, so can Jesus. Help your child understand and experience the love and constancy of Jesus.

81. What if my spouse is not a believer and is not interested in spiritually nurturing our child?

Although it can be difficult and confusing for kids when they receive mixed messages from their parents about who God is and whether or not we need a Savior,

Judy Cook points out that the early learning years offer wonderful opportunities for faith nurture because young children love to hear God's stories, accept what they're taught about prayer and about having a relationship with Jesus, and are often willing to happily attend church with you.

Things can become a little more complicated once children hit the preteen years and may feel drawn towards the religious views of the other parent. Cook points out that as children question their own identity during their teen years, they will also test what you and the other parent have taught them about God. During this time you'll need to be patient and extend grace. Cook says, "You have taught your children about God as you experience and love him, and now is the time to give them over to God and the leading of the Holy Spirit, while staying alert to any invitation from your children that can nurture their faith."

When you're giving your teen child time and space to explore her relationship with God, Cook cautions against entering a power struggle with your spouse about what your child can and can't do where religion is concerned. Instead, let your child express her ideas about God and faith—even if they are painful to hear—and allow her to stay home if she isn't willing to accompany you to church anymore. According to

Cook, allowing your child to explore the other side of belief in God in an atmosphere of respect both for your faith and the other parent's non-faith gives your child the room she needs to remember what you taught during childhood.

Finally, remember that even though you may be raising your child to know God without the support or encouragement of the other parent, you are *not* alone—God is on this journey with you.

82. What should I do if I am not married to the other parent and that parent has different standards regarding religion than I do?

It's painful when your child belongs to two households and the parent in one of those households does not share your beliefs. However, as Judy Cook explains, kids are very good at adapting to different circumstances—even when that involves a Christian family setting and one that's non-Christian or less religious.

The problems arise for kids when parents are in conflict with each other over lifestyle choices, religious beliefs, or parenting styles. It's with that in mind that Cook points out, "Unless your children need protection from the other parent's abusive or neglectful behavior (i.e., if the other parent is alcohol or drug addicted, or is physically, emotionally, or sexually abusive or married to someone with such dysfunctions), you cannot make demands or set rules for your children in someone else's household."

Concentrate on your sphere of influence—your home—by making the most of your time with your child and building a strong relationship of love and trust. Reflect God's love to your child and provide him with security and warmth. Be respectful when you talk about or with the other parent, and let your child know it's necessary for him to live under two sets of rules and beliefs. "And," says Cook, "help him experience that when he spends time in your home, love rules."

83. My child is adopted—how should we talk about it?

The stories of our families help shape our identity; they're part of our personal journey. When part of your child's personal journey involves the loss of a birth parent through famine or AIDS or other tragic death, or relinquishment or legal termination of parental rights, your child will need to talk about it.

As an adoptive parent you can help most with that conversation.

"Adoptive families are formed out of loss," says Ron Nydam. There may be a deep-down grief in your child's heart about starting out in life with the personal injury of first-parent loss, even as a baby. In order to bring *your* heart to the places in the heart of your child where there is the most suffering, you need to talk about the loss of birth parents as part of the adoptive family story. Help your child form his identity by taking the lead on finding and offering information and by being open to your child's birth family story and family culture. Make your conversations inclusive by using the words "adoptive family" as your primary descriptor, rather than "adopted child."

Be aware that the conversations you have together may include sadness, wondering, and fantasy about lost parents. Give your child space to be sad as he figures these things out.

"All these things," says Nydam, "will help with the most important variable in adoption, namely, the degree to which a child adopts his adoptive parents, forming deep attachment. The strength of this relationship is the foundation for a healthy personality and a hearty trust in God."

84. How do I help kids trust God when they're worried?

Although *we* know when worries like monsters, tests, and thunderstorms are irrational or beyond our control, many kids don't. Teaching them to rely on God in the midst of their worries is a wonderful reminder that God cares about the details of their lives and is with them every step of the way.

Talk to God together when your child is stressed about something. Pray with your child, asking God to help her when she's afraid of monsters (or bugs or the first day of school) and thanking God for promising to care for her. Make up a tune to an encouraging passage of Scripture together that your child can call upon in stressful times. (For my kids, that verse is "When I am afraid I will trust in you" from Psalm 56:3, sung to a tune written by Frank Hernandez and recorded by Steve Green.)

You can also encourage your child by sharing stories of God's faithfulness. Read the story of Noah together and then imagine Noah's thoughts as he built the ark: "What if I'm not done in time?" "How will I shut the door if I'm inside?" Check out the story of Moses and the burning bush and consider Moses' anxiety when God told him to bring Pharaoh a message: "What if everyone laughs at me?" Read about

Rahab and wonder how she clung to God's protection promise while the walls of Jericho crashed down around her.

Be sure to tell about times in your own life when you experienced God's care. Remind your kids that God is faithful to them just as he was to Noah, Moses, Rahab, and you!

85. How do I tell kids the truth about difficult situations?

Although our natural inclination as a parent might be to protect our child by *not* telling the truth, Jan Talen says it's vital that we *do*. As she points out, "Lying to or withholding the truth from children breaks trust at a time when their emotions and sense of security may already be stretched."

It's important to tell the truth in an age-appropriate way so the child will gain positive skills and understanding through the experience. Talen offers these suggestions to help you share the truth in difficult situations:

- Settle your own anger and upset feelings first, so that you pass as little of that on to your child as possible. (Your child should not feel that it's her task to take care of you or to calm you down.)

- Prioritize what you think your child needs to know. Avoid sharing too many details or assigning blame.

- Plan a time to talk when your child is calm, not too hungry or tired, and when she'll have the time and space afterwards to mull things over in her own way.

- Tell the truth in short sentences—about as many sentences as the child's age.

- Invite your child to say back to you what she has heard, and encourage her to ask questions.

- Later, touch base with your child again so she can ask other questions or share thoughts.

- Show your child a written plan of how you (as the adult) will be handling the situation, and list specific things that might be happening. For example, if you are sharing that a family member has cancer, you might write down the plan for treatment, the dates that treatment will occur, specific details about how that might impact your child's schedule and what adjustments you'll make, and so on.

- Reassure your child through your words and perhaps through God's words that everything will be OK, even if you are not sure what OK looks like right now.

86. How do I help my child when he fails?

On April 25, 2003, thirteen-year-old Natalie Gilbert was singing the national anthem during an NBA game between the Portland Trail Blazers and the Dallas Mavericks when she forgot the words. Her one shining moment seemed destined for failure as she stood there uncertain, anxious, and verging on tears—until Maurice Cheeks, coach of the Trail Blazers, walked across the floor and stood beside her. He put an arm around her shoulder, helped her raise the microphone back up, and began singing the words she had forgotten. He remained there until the end of the song, coaching her through it, singing louder when she faltered, and softer as she gained her confidence back.

It's a given that your kids will fail occasionally. Your job is to coach them through their failures. Coaches don't play the game for their players; they demonstrate the skills their players need to know before sending them off to try them out. Your child needs to know that failure is part of learning. Tell your child about your failures, how you worked through disappointment and how you grew. Let your child know that you love him even when he isn't

> The picture book *Koala Lou* by Mem Fox is a wonderful story of failure and a mother's lasting love.

"the best." And give your child a skill-set that includes the knowledge that God is walking beside him every day and loves him even when he fails.

87. How do I teach my child to rely on God?

An online search of the words "fully rely on God" will yield pages upon pages of bright green frogs bearing the "F.R.O.G." acronym on a wide array of paraphernalia for purchase. While F.R.O.G. gizmos and gadgets are fun reminders about relying on God, a catchy acronym isn't enough to teach your child that truth. Relying on God requires learning by doing and, since childhood (and parenting) is filled with uncertain times and new experiences, there are lots of opportunities to practice! Try these:

- Turn difficult experiences—a stay in the hospital, the first day of school, moving to a new neighborhood, being caught in a storm, dealing with divorce, feeling left out, and more—into teachable moments by pausing for prayer and remembering that God is always with us.

- Share stories of how God provided for others. The Noah family had to rely on God while building the ark and living in it; Joseph had to rely on God while waiting for rescue at the bottom of a well; Mary had to rely on God for a place to rest when there was no room at the inn. Read the stories about the people in God's family—and be sure to share stories of your own!

- Learn some of God's promises from Scripture together and encourage your child to call on those passages in times of worry. When our girls were little we used to sing, "When I am afraid I will trust in you" from Psalm 56:3 to the tune sung by recording artist Steve Green. They and I still sing that song in times of uncertainty. Some other great verses to learn: Matthew 19:26, Joshua 1:9, and Jeremiah 29:11.

Fun resources to help you memorize Scripture and the books of the Bible together:
www.whatsinthebible.com
www.stevegreenministries.org
www.seedsfamilyworship.net

88. How do I make wise decisions when it comes to my child's use of technology?

When our fourth child, Tara, turned twelve, we inadvertently put the whole world in her hands. After carefully raising her three older siblings through each technological advancement and doing all the things experts told us to do—keep the computer in the kitchen, keep the TV out of kids' bedrooms, limit playing time on gaming devices—we got careless. We jumped at the chance to skip shopping when Tara offered to contribute her piggy bank funds and pay for half the cost of an iPod Touch as her birthday gift. Having done no research, we were shocked to discover that it came with free wireless, impossible-for-us-to-block Internet access.

In an article on www.nurturekidsfaith.org, Dean Heetderks provides tips to help you and your kids keep technology in perspective. He shares advice like this:

- It's OK to say no to the latest technologies—even when your child says everyone else owns it and they'll die if they don't have it. Everyone doesn't, and your child won't.

- Keep technology (including a TV) out of your child's bedroom and in a public space in your home. You need to know what they are viewing and to whom they are communicating.

- Set clear limits when it comes to technology use: no cell phones in your room at night, homework before computer games, ask permission before using, and so on.

- Get involved and stay involved with what your child is using by playing the games they are playing and staying abreast of the technology they are using.

- Find out what the games, technology, and rules are at their friends' homes. Talk about what your kids could do if their friends' family rules are different from yours.

- Encourage your child to show you what he can do with technology—your child will be proud to teach you something and you will stay informed.

- Set a good example. Do you limit your own use of technology at home? Are you able to ignore your cell phone to finish the conversation you're having with your child? Do you shut your Blackberry off during your child's soccer game? Don't let technology take the place of face-to-face family interaction.

- Teach your child that the same rules of respect you observe when interacting with others at home and away from home apply to the way they interact with others when using technology. That means that technology is not a tool for sharing gossip, saying hurtful things, or bullying.

- Be safe. The Internet really is a window to the world—all that's good and all that's bad. You wouldn't let young children play in a park unattended; don't let them play in cyberspace alone either. Know your kids' usernames and passwords, and monitor the sites they visit. Teach them not to share information with strangers. Invest in a good monitoring system that will block access to dangerous sites, then check and update it often.

- Encourage your kids to tell you any time they discover something inappropriate online, and then stay calm as you figure out together how it got there and how to get rid of it. (If your children anticipate a bad reaction from you they'll be less likely to tell you.)

CHAPTER **6**

TIME, TALENTS, AND TITHES

Recently I waited at a red light behind a car covered with bumper stickers that read: "Make Love, Not War," "Give Peace a Chance," and "What Part of KILL Don't You Understand?" While it's probably safe to assume that the car's owner has strong feelings about peace and war, having bumper stickers on his or her car doesn't mean that the driver is actually involved in peacekeeping.

As a kid I attended a girls' club at my church. Each week we were asked, "What does the Lord require of

> GOD told Abram: "Leave your country, your family, and your father's home for a land that I will show you. I'll make you a great nation and bless you. I'll make you famous; you'll be a blessing. I'll bless those who bless you; those who curse you I'll curse. All the families of the Earth will be blessed through you."
>
> Genesis 12:1-3, *The Message*

you?" We answered, "To do justice, love kindness, and walk humbly with our God. Micah 6:8." We all knew the verse by heart then, and it's probably safe to assume that most of us can still recite it by heart now. But just because we knew the words doesn't mean we were actually living justly, spreading kindness, and practicing humility.

We can tell our kids that there are people living in poverty in our city and around the world, we can watch TV together and see the effects of natural disasters on people's lives, and we can explain that there are diseases for which there's no known cure, but when it comes to poverty and suffering and pain, *knowledge is not enough.*

Many years ago God came to a man named Abram and set up a covenant with him. Abram got the best end of the arrangement: God promised to bless him and his descendants beyond their wildest dreams and called them to bless others. As God's people we've been offered that same incredible deal and are called to live out our faith in the same way.

As parents we're helping to shape the faith of our children when we "walk the talk" together. Ask God to show you where your family can be a blessing. Think about how you can use your time, talents, and tithes together. Then roll up your sleeves and go.

Questions
89. How do I teach my child to be a good steward of God's creation?

I probably shouldn't admit this, but I don't like having to use the little green compost bin that sits under my kitchen sink. I resent the extra step on the garbage trail, I don't like the space it takes up in an already crowded cupboard, and I hate the smell. My kids, on the other hand, who are growing up in a world where it's cool to be "green," gasp in horror if they catch me throwing something compostable into the regular garbage!

The best way to encourage your kids to practice good stewardship is to live it as a family. Lead by example, and be sure to follow your kids' lead too! It's also important that you share the "why" behind the daily choices your family makes as caretakers of the planet and its resources. Taking good care of our world is our God-given responsibility and a way to demonstrate our gratitude to God. (Remember that the next time it's your turn to stir the compost bin!)

15 Family-friendly stewardship ideas

- Compost everything you can.
- Turn off lights and electronics when not in use.
- Conserve water by turning off the tap while brushing teeth.
- Pack lunches in reusable containers.
- Drink from refillable water bottles.
- Recycle cans, jars, plastic bottles, and paper products.
- Buy locally grown food and items marked "fair trade" whenever possible.
- Reuse paper before recycling it. (**Tip:** Make notepads from scrap paper together.)
- Walk, bike, or use public transit.
- Wash your car with a bucket of water instead of spraying it with a hose.
- Visit thrift stores to shop and to donate items.
- Plant a tree.
- Pick up garbage.
- Hang clothes outside to dry.
- Buy items with less packaging.

90. How do I teach my child to share what she has?

As you encourage your child to share, keep in mind that what you're asking her to do isn't always easy, especially for young children. Help your child get a handle on sharing with these ideas:

- Make sharing an enjoyable experience by not forcing your child to share a treasured toy. Before a guest arrives, let your child know she can put away one or two really special things if she doesn't think she's ready to share them yet.

- Share with your child—slice up an apple and share the pieces, divide up a piece of cake, take turns blowing bubbles outside, bounce a ball back and forth, take turns playing a computer game. Point out how fun sharing can be!

- Have games, toys, and craft supplies in your home that belong to the family instead of just one person.

- Share with others together. Prepare a tray of veggies to eat with friends, help your child make a card and mail it to someone, select food from your cupboard together and deliver it to the food bank.

- Be patient. Understand that the ability to share improves with maturity. (Junior probably won't engage in a tug of war over the blue marker when he's eleven.) Keep encouraging your child to share, but don't feel like a bad parent when your two-year-old ends a play date with a tantrum!

91. How do I encourage my child to want to help others?

When our daughter Kailey was three, she toted a pink blanket everywhere. She wore it around her head, draped it over her shoulders, scrunched it into the basket on the front of her tricycle, and dragged it down the aisle when she was a flower girl. She even named it "Mine." Soon, we were calling it Mine too. On those frightening occasions when it went missing, we'd run through the house with parental panic rising in our voices, yelling, "Has anyone see Mine? Where's Mine?"

When you're a preschooler, life is all about "mine." But often that's our tendency as adults too. However, as Jesus-followers we know we're called to move beyond ourselves and "do justice, love kindness, and walk humbly with our God" (Mic. 6:8).

In order to raise compassionate kids—those who recognize suffering and feel compelled to extend lovingkindness—we need to live compassionate lives ourselves. In order to encourage your child to want to help others, he needs to see you speaking out against injustice, sharing what you have, being a friend to those in need, and treating others with dignity and respect. Show your child that as imagebearers of God all people are "wonderfully made" (Ps. 139:14) and of equal worth.

It's also important that kids have opportunities to share with and help others. Take your child along when you bring someone a meal, sort and donate old clothes and toys together, include her when you volunteer for a cause, and practice random acts of kindness together. Pray regularly with each other about people in need and for those in charge and ask God to show you ways to help.

92. How do I teach my child to be inclusive and welcoming to everyone?

When it comes to being inclusive and welcoming, kids are taking their cues from us. Some important things to keep in mind:

- Be positive. Let your kids hear you say positive things about other people. Demonstrate love in the way you treat and interact with people you know and those you don't know.

- Expand your circle of friends. Fight your natural instinct to gravitate toward folks who look like you or who share your tax bracket. Get to know the other parents from your child's teams, clubs, and class at school.

- Practice empathy. Invite your child to consider how he would feel and how he would want to be helped if he were the new kid on the team or the person who wasn't invited to the party. Discuss how to include others when on the playground, in the neighborhood, and in Sunday school.

- Discuss differences. Recent studies show that kids aren't "colorblind" when it comes to race. Instead, they categorize people based on what they can see: skin color, hair, weight, and so on, and they tend to prefer kids who look and act like they do. Instead of ignoring differences or shushing your child when he or she makes an inappropriate comment, talk about equality—racial and other-wise—in the same way you teach your child about gender equality.

- Be aware. Monitor and discuss the TV shows and movies your child is watching and the computer games he or she is playing—do they make fun of a person's pain (often the case in reality shows) or portray a particular group of people as the "bad guys"?

- Share the stories. When Jesus walked this earth he went out of his way to connect with folks who felt excluded. He risked being ostracized and criticized to befriend people like Zacchaeus, Matthew, and a Samaritan woman. Jesus also told stories to illustrate God's love for everyone in his kingdom. Use those stories to jump-start some great discussions on showing that love to others.

93. How do I teach my child to share with people who are less fortunate without giving money indiscriminately or inappropriately to strangers?

For the most part, incorporating the "Golden Rule" into the values we instill in our kids isn't that difficult. We discourage greed and encourage sharing. We involve them in loving others when we help a neighbor by raking leaves or shoveling snow. We encourage our kids to be respectful. We teach that being a bystander to bullying is wrong.

Things become a little less clear when "loving our neighbor" takes us out of our comfort zone. What happens when our kids start to ask questions for which we have no easy answers? *We* know that handing money to a person who is homeless may not always provide the most loving solution to his problems, but *our kids* see money as an obvious solution. After all, we taught them to share, right?

There are going to be times when God presents us with encounters that will take us out of our comfort zones. Don't avoid talking about those situations; instead, use them as teachable moments in which you can wonder together about how God might want you to respond.

For example, here are some things to consider when discussing homelessness with your child:

- Use respectful language—instead of "that homeless guy," say, "the man who is homeless."

- Avoid making judgments about the person's situation.

- Explain to your child that there are many reasons why people become homeless. Loss of a job, unaffordable housing, illness, addiction, and family problems are just a few possible causes.

- Help your child understand that people of all ages, genders, ethnicities, and religions can become homeless and that they have names, families, and favorite things just like you and your child do.

- If you opt not to give money or food directly to someone, talk with your child about better ways to help. Follow up with actions such as donating clothes, food, or other items to a shelter; volunteering together; and speaking up about issues relating to homelessness in your community.

- Pray together for the person you saw and regularly include those without homes in your family prayers.

- Visit the local library for age-appropriate books on homelessness and learn more together.

Picture books on homelessness

Fly Away Home by Eve Bunting

Uncle Willie and the Soup Kitchen by Dyanne DiSalvo-Ryan

A Shelter in Our Car by Monica Gunning

---

94. What do I say when my child asks why some people are rich and some people are poor?

Begin by saying, "That's a great question," and then delve a little deeper to discover what triggered it: "What got you wondering about rich and poor people?" Chances are that your child has a specific situation in mind. Maybe he's frustrated that his buddy has a new technology that he doesn't have. Maybe her bus passed a homeless man on the way to school this morning. Or maybe a commercial about kids in a developing country came on between cartoons yesterday. Finding out what triggered the question will help you determine the best way to respond.

Then focus on what's at the heart of your child's question. Keep your answer simple and end with a faith response. Something like this: "Things aren't always fair. Because sin is in the world, bad things happen in people's lives. God knows that some people have a lot and some people have only a little. So what do you think God wants us to do?"

Questions like these provide a great opportunity for your family to live out your faith! So brainstorm ideas and then do something together. (You'll find lots of ideas in this chapter!)

95. How do I make giving real and meaningful for my child?

Kids are hands-on learners! The more "real" the cause is to them, the more meaningful the giving experience will be. The following list contains some practical ideas to get you started:

- Invite your child to select and purchase food for the food bank, then deliver it there together. (While you're there, find out if you can come back and help by stocking shelves.)

- Sort old clothes together and bring them to a thrift shop that uses the profits to help others in the community.

- Help your child understand where money collected at church is going each week by looking online at images and information about the cause a particular offering supports.

- Enter a walk-a-thon or bike-a-thon together.

- Make a "Giving Jar" to collect coins, and include your child in choosing the cause you'll be giving the money to when it's full.

- Volunteer at an animal shelter together.

- Select a cause to support together and then provide your child with opportunities to earn money around the house to make the donation.

- Set up a lemonade stand or host a garage sale, then donate the proceeds or use the money to purchase something specific for those in need.

- React when natural disaster strikes by discussing and deciding on a way to help: making financial donations, organizing a fundraiser, collecting needed supplies, and praying are just a few ideas.

- Visit the website of a denominational ministry and look for practical ways you can help others. For example, ministries working in developing countries might suggest the purchase of a goat, school or medical supplies, mosquito nets, or a bicycle. Find out what your child would like to buy, then come up with a way to earn, save, and donate the money together.

96. Should I make my child give his own money to church or charity?

Although your child may look at you like you've just asked him to donate a body part, the answer is yes, Junior should give some of his own money to church or charity. Passing a child pocket change to put in the offering plate isn't very different from handing him a coin to place in a bubble- gum machine. Kids learn more about the value of money when they spend their own. In the case of church offerings, they may also learn more about the value of giving.

While the general rule of thumb when it comes to giving is a tithe of 10 percent (or more), our goal as parents is not to teach kids to obey the letter of the law, but to create in their hearts both an understanding that everything they have is a gift from God and a desire to share those gifts with others.

As in so many other areas, showing is better than telling. Leonard Vander Zee recalls that as a child his parents had an envelope system for budgeting, and everyone knew the first one to get filled was the tithe envelope. Share with your child about how, what, and why you give.

> What is important for kids to learn is that no matter how much money they have, earn, win, or inherit, they need to know how to spend it, how to save it, and how to give it to others in need.
>
> —Barbara Coloroso, *Kids Are Worth It!*, Penguin 2001, pp. 245-246. Used by permission.

97. How much should my kids know about my finances?

When my teens ask me for cash, I usually suggest that they run outside and pick some off the money tree. They roll their eyes, but they understand what I'm saying. With younger children the old money tree suggestion doesn't work very well; they need some help in understanding the world of finance.

So does that mean you should open your wallet, show them your paycheck, and take them along to your next bank meeting? No, but there are a few things they should know as fellow members of your family.

- You budget and plan for purchases. There's a reason you can't instantly spring for the latest tech toy—it's not in the budget.

- You make choices based on wants and needs. That means sometimes you choose not to buy or do something even though it's within your financial means.

- Your credit card and debit card purchases aren't "free," but need to be paid back.

- You set aside money regularly to give back to God— for church and for other local and global causes.

- Your children are not to blame for any financial struggles you might have.

- You will always do your best to provide for their needs.
- Your level of happiness is not based on your level of income.

98. How often should my family volunteer?

For some families, donating time to a specific organization together—dog walking at the animal shelter, visiting residents at a retirement home, and so on—works well; for others it makes more sense to simply seek out practical ways to show love to others while responding to needs as they arise: shoveling snow for a neighbor or making a meal for a new mom, for example. The main thing is that your kids know that you do more than *talk about* and *experience* God's love—you *extend it* too.

99. Do all our service projects have to be church-related?

No. While it's important to find ways that your family can participate and serve as members of your church family, God has also placed your family in a larger community. It's important to discover how you can be used by God there too!

100. What kind of service projects are appropriate to do as a family?

Consider children's gifts and areas of interest when selecting service projects your family can do together. For example, a musical child might sing or play an instrument at a retirement home, while the family math whiz would prefer to do puzzles with the residents. A social child will enjoy interacting with guests at a shelter, while an artistic child might prefer to create a card to give away.

> Now that I, your Lord and Teacher, have washed your feet, you also should wash one another's feet. I have set you an example that you should do as I have done for you.
>
> —John 13:14-15

Look for age-appropriate ways that everyone can participate. Small children can sort and carry objects, smile and entertain others, and enjoy the ride at a bike-a-thon. Older children can take on bigger responsibilities; encourage them by letting them run with their ideas.

Here are ten ideas for service projects that all ages will enjoy:

- Be part of a church Vacation Bible School team. Distribute invitations, make snacks, teach a class, prepare crafts, and so on.

- Invite another family (or families) to do a service scavenger hunt with you. Make a list of specific ways to serve—pick up garbage, sweep a sidewalk, smile at a shopper, pray for someone who looks unhappy, find five things to pray about, help somebody, and so on—and reunite afterwards to share stories.

- Adopt a park or a nearby street and pick up garbage together.

- Bake something together and give it away to a neighbor, a new mom, or someone else you know.

- Visit a nursing home. **Tip:** Ask if you can bring a well-behaved dog or cat to visit too!

- Go shopping together for inexpensive items—socks, toiletries, kids' craft supplies—then package and donate them to a shelter.

- Help out at an animal shelter.

- Participate in a walk-a-thon, bike-a-thon, or fun-run to support a cause you care about.

- Volunteer at a conversation circle for adults and children who are learning English as a second language.

- Volunteer together at your local YMCA. **Tip:** Find out if they have a host family program where your family will be matched with a family who's new to North America.

CHAPTER **7**

THE CHURCH FAMILY

Our firstborn, Steph, was born with "hip dysplasia" — a fancy term that means she was born with a severely dislocated hip. At her baptism the pastor shared with the congregation that in order to prepare her muscles for surgery the following week, Steph was going to spend seven days lying on her back with her little legs pulled up in the air and strapped to a bar placed across the width of her crib.

In the days that followed, our church family made sure we felt God's presence in our lives by being present

> Then Jesus' mother and brothers arrived. Standing outside, they sent someone in to call him. A crowd was sitting around him, and they told him, "Your mother and brothers are outside looking for you." "Who are my mother and my brothers?" he asked. Then he looked at those seated in a circle around him and said, "Here are my mother and my brothers! Whoever does God's will is my brother and sister and mother."
>
> —Mark 3:31-35

themselves. One member arrived at our door and offered to sit beside Steph's crib for a few hours and then slipped money into my hand, telling Ron and me to go get some ice cream together. Another came to bring a meal and then stayed so I could rest. A senior member of the congregation sent a note, promising to pray. And, hours after we arrived home from the surgery, our pastor showed up with a single red rose and said, "I know you're tired, I won't stay; I just want you to know I've been praying and am here if you need anything."

A year or so after Steph's surgery we moved to a new city several hours away. Although we've only been back in that church a handful of times in the twenty years since, on each occasion a member of that church—our church family—has approached one of us and said, "Is that the same little girl who had that surgery when she was a baby? I remember praying for her. What a blessing that she is so healthy now!"

Jesus once looked around at the crowd of believers surrounding him and told them they were his family. The crowd of believers that surrounds you in church on Sunday are *your* family. Faith nurture is too big a job for parents to accomplish alone. We need the help of the whole church, and at baptism that's what your church family promises to do. We're all in this together.

Questions
101. How do I find a church that will nurture my child's faith?

Have you ever seen a mom try to leave a church nursery while a screaming child clings to her leg like Velcro? That was me. Three of my four kids were clingers (I'd mastered the art of "drop off and run" by the time the fourth one came along). If you'd have asked me back then what I was looking for in a church, I probably would have answered, "A place my kids like going."

Important? Sure, but when you're seeking a church that will nurture your child's faith (and your own!), you want to look for a congregation where all ages are valued, accepted, and included in the whole life of the church. When searching for a church where your child's faith will be nurtured, keep these questions in mind:

- Does this church provide children with opportunities to regularly experience and participate in congregational worship?

- Does this church provide children with the opportunity to worship, wonder, and learn with each other in developmentally appropriate ways?

- Does this church value and accept children as *current* members of the church family, rather than treating them as though they are in training to be members *someday*?

- Does this church provide opportunities for intergenerational relationships in which people of all ages can share faith stories and ask questions together?

- Does this church provide opportunities for children to share and respond to God's love by serving others?

- If you are already a member of a church, but are dissatisfied with its family-friendliness, think of the suggestions above as things to work toward right where you are. Talk to the pastor or other church leaders about your concerns and offer to help work toward solutions.

102. Why should I take my child to church?

All four of my kids play basketball. Although our youngest, Tara, was toted along to all of her siblings' games, wore their jerseys, and grew up in a home with a ball in every corner, that's not how she learned the game. Tara learned the game by *playing*. It wasn't until she joined a team, picked up a ball, dribbled it down the floor, and banked a shot off the backboard that she truly experienced basketball.

Children learn through observation, but they learn best through participation. We take them to church so that being part of a church family and gathering regularly to worship God in community with others becomes part of the fabric of their lives.

103. What if my child doesn't want to go to church?

Find out why. Is it simply a case of early-morning rebellion, or does your child have a legitimate concern? Once you know the reason behind the resistance, you can work toward a solution. Here are some things to consider:

- If your child is young and is choosing church attendance as a way to exert his independence, you may want to offer some choices that will allow him to feel autonomous and help you arrive on time. Asking, "Would you like to wear the blue shirt or the red shirt?" might be enough to refocus your child's attention and keep him moving.

- If you discover that your child is having difficulty with another child or adult at your church, take her concerns seriously and do some problem-solving together.

- If your very young child is fearful of staying behind in the nursery, remain there with her a few times or begin by leaving her for a brief time before returning to pick her up so she understands you won't be gone forever. When possible, connect with the nursery providers so they know if and when it's time to take over.

- Don't worry too much if your church's children's ministry program is offered during the worship service and your child prefers to stay in church with you. Spending time worshiping with you is also a great place for her to be!

When your child enters what Ron Nydam refers to as the "push-pull of adolescence" and resists going to church, an open conversation about his spiritual experience is important. As Nydam points out, "Worship is about dialogue and conversation with God. Not wanting to go to a service of public worship is a good opportunity for talking about the faith of both the parent and the child." Compromise might be the best solution here. For example, a child may have a choice in *where* he attends worship, but not *whether* he attends.

Nydam reminds us that while church attendance is an important family value, it's not a goal in itself. "The goal must always be a young heart where the law and love of God reside."

Finally, a word about wardrobe—while church *attendance* might not be negotiable when your child is young, what she *wears* might be. For example, allowing your four-year-old the freedom to wear her prized cowboy boots, plastic tiara, and favorite flower girl dress to church allows her independence and freedom of expression as she personally prepares for worship. (And don't worry, she won't be going to church dressed like that when she's thirty!)

104. How do I explain to my child what worship at church is all about?

Kids know all about parties and special occasions, so begin by explaining that the worship service at your church is a special celebration for God every week. Point out that worship is all about *God*, not *us*. It's our opportunity to gather together with other people in God's family and give thanks and praise to God, talk to and listen to God, remember and hear God's story, and bring God our offerings.

105. How do I help my child prepare for worship at church?

"Time to go! Where's my purse? I don't have any clean socks! Can you please comb your hair? I'll be in the car! Grab the diaper bag! Wait—I forgot my wallet! I thought I asked you to comb your hair! OK, let's go! Stop—do you smell something?"

Sound familiar? One of the most important ways you can prepare your child (and yourself) for worship is to remove stress from your Sunday mornings. Here's how:

- Choose and set out clothes the night before. **Tip:** Be sure your child knows that her appearance doesn't matter to God and it shouldn't matter to those in your congregation. Keep the focus on worship, not wardrobe, by inviting your child to choose and wear decent, comfortable clothes.

- Get up early so you have plenty of time to get ready.

- Keep breakfast simple and special. Serve a treat like a favorite cereal, mini-muffins, coffee cake, or fruit and yogurt in a special bowl.

- Use the words "We're going to worship" instead of "We're going to church."

- Hang a copy of the weekly church bulletin on the refrigerator so you'll know—and be able to talk about—what will be happening on Sunday *before* Sunday comes. Tell your child what the offering will support so he or she can consider what to give. Wonder aloud about how the message title relates to the content, and try to include the Scripture passage in a family devotion time.

- Play music that glorifies God as you get ready together and on the way to worship.

- Let your child see from your attitude that going to church is something to look forward to. (In her book *Parenting in the Pew,* author Robbie Castleman shares how she used to set the tone by telling her kids, "Jesus must be excited! This is his special day!").

106. How do I make worship a meaningful experience for my kids?

When I was a child, my dad would pass peppermints to me and my brothers midway through the service. My agile mother-in-law managed to keep her arms folded and her eyes on the minister while quietly pinching her four wiggly sons into submission during the sermon. My friend used to bring a bag filled with toys to occupy her kids—until the day her twins attempted to race a pair of Hot Wheels down the aisle during the offertory. Although these child management techniques may win high marks for creativity, it's safe to say they didn't go a long way toward making worship meaningful!

We know it's important for kids to experience and participate in worship with their church family, but it's easy for them to become bored when there's much opportunity to move around or when things are hard to understand. As you're looking for ways to make worship meaningful for your child, it's helpful to imagine that *you* are your child and view things from his or her perspective. Here are some other things to keep in mind:

- Get a good view. Your child is much more likely to pay attention if she can actually see what's happening, so choose the front row instead of the back. **Tip:** Young kids may also appreciate sitting on a booster seat.

- Point out what is happening. Draw your child's attention to the PowerPoint image on the screen, point to the words as you read Scripture, and help him follow along with the order of worship, explaining any difficult words. Resist the temptation to "shush" his questions!

- Invite participation. Encourage your child to sing along by pointing out a repeated phrase or chorus she can join in on. Bring some sticky notes and ask your child to mark the songs you'll be singing in the songbook and/or the passage you'll be reading in the Bible. Invite your child to put some of her own money in the offering plate and talk about who the money will support.

- Continue at home. Reflect on what happened during church when you're at home. For example, connect the baptism you witnessed with a story about the day your child was baptized, wonder aloud about the liturgical art in the sanctuary, and sing a song you learned together.

107. How do I explain the sacraments to my child?

When I was little, my brothers and I would sneak a mint in our mouths at the moment all the adults ate their communion bread in church. Although I knew the white cubes of bread had been prepared by my grandfather at his bakery, I imagined that they must taste special and very different from the loaves my dad brought home from work.

Kids wonder about the things they see. While most churchgoing kids aren't able to remember their own baptism, they've seen countless others. Until your child experiences tasting the bread and juice at the Lord's Table, they'll wonder what's going on with that too.

Begin to help your child understand the sacrament of baptism and the Lord's Table by explaining that sacraments are things God gives us to remind and assure us that we belong to him and that Jesus loves us and died and rose again for us. We celebrate the sacraments in church with all of God's people, and we need them to help us remember that God is good and loving. The sacraments also make us happy and thankful to be God's people!

Build on your child's understanding of baptism by asking if he knows what baptism means and why it's important. Make it personal by asking, "Do you know why *you* were baptized?" Then tell your child the story of his baptism—the time, the place, who was there, and why everyone was so happy! Share with your child that when he was baptized, God promised to forgive his sins and send his Spirit to help him. At your child's baptism God said, "You are my child, part of my family, the church!"

Introduce your child to the Lord's Table by explaining that when God's people, old and young, share in communion, God is calling us to remember Jesus and how he died on the cross and rose again so that our sins would be forgiven. Share with a young child that the bread and wine/juice help us remember that Jesus was hurt and died because he loved us. An older child will be able to understand how the elements represent Jesus' body and blood, and how receiving them assures us that Jesus' sacrifice covers our sins. As your child grows in faith, her understanding of what is happening and what it represents will take on a deeper level of meaning, just as it has for you.

108. What should my role as a parent be in the church?

I'm passionate about children's ministry and have been involved in children's programs at church since I was a teen. There's no place I'd rather be on a Sunday morning than sharing God's story while sitting on the floor with a group of seven-year-olds. But when our children were young there was a period of time when my commitment to children's ministry caused Sunday morning chaos in our home. I was overwhelmed trying to meet the needs of my church and my children. I should have said no to spending too many hours in ministry involvement and yes to more quality time with my family, myself, and God. The program would have been fine without me, and I know God would have understood.

While it's important that you use the gifts God has given you and that you model what it means to be part of the body of Christ, the faith nurture of your family—and you!—has to be a priority. Sometimes that means scaling back on what you used to do until your family requires less of you.

In the meantime, strike a balance by looking for areas in your church where you could serve together and where you can limit the hours of time that are required. If you have a marriage partner, support each other by taking turns with your level of involvement.

109. Is it important that my child interacts with the adults in our church?

Incredibly important! If we want our children to view the church as their extended family and to see themselves as valued members of that family, we need to help them connect in meaningful ways with others in that community.

Having been a teen and young adult yourself, you probably know that there will come a time when your child won't be taking her cues only from you. During those years it's especially important that your child has relationships with other adults who can encourage her in her walk with God. Those relationships can begin now, when your child is young.

> Giving children and teens the opportunity to make a real contribution to their church is indeed important, but more important than this are the connections that they make with the people with whom they interact. Relationships have a more lasting impact than programs.
>
> —Robert J. Keeley, *Helping our Children Grow in Faith,* Baker 2008, p. 35. Used by permission.

110. How do I know if a church is providing a safe environment for children?

When I was a child, providing a safe church environment for children involved replacing broken nursery toys. Thankfully, in addition to making sure that toys meet national safety standards and being more proactive in providing allergy-safe zones, many churches are also actively involved in creating environments that keep children safe from sexual abuse. To find out if your church—or a church you're visiting—is doing the latter, Beth Swagman says to look for these three things:

- A child safety policy that includes specific policy statements about how to keep kids safe in each ministry program (for example, in a church with few kids there should be a plan for how to group the kids and how the leaders are supervised); screening of church workers through interviews, references, and a criminal record check; and details about how to handle a report of suspected abuse. A church environment won't be safe if wrongdoers aren't reported.

- Annual educational events about child abuse that are offered for church workers, staff, and parents. As Swagman points out, "A church environment is safer when members know what abuse is, can recognize its signs and symptoms, know the steps to reduce the risk, and work together to prevent abuse from occurring."

- Visible signs that the church has taken steps to create a safer space. Classrooms should have windows in the doors so people can see inside. The nursery should be located near the sanctuary, not tucked away in a basement. Young children should have quick washroom access. (A washroom in the nursery is ideal.)

111. How do I approach my church family about including my special-needs child?

Hopefully you won't have to approach your church family about including your special-needs child any more than the parent of a child without a disability would have to advocate for that child. However, if your church seems uncertain about how to best serve your child, Nella Uitvlugt suggests the following:

- Meet with the pastor and church educator to begin a dialogue and to set up a spiritual formation plan or a spiritual IEP (Individual Education Plan), the goal of which is for the child to be successful in the least restrictive environment possible. Depending on the child's age and developmental level, it might also be appropriate to invite the childcare provider from the nursery, the Sunday school teacher, the youth leader, a peer buddy, and a special education teacher.

• Discuss things like these: What does the child enjoy? What is the child gifted at/in? What causes distress or stress? Are there any medical issues of which the child's ministry leader(s) should be made aware? How should one redirect behavior if needed? Are there any behaviors that might be harmful to other children or that might cause other children to be afraid? If so, what causes the behavior to escalate and are there ways this can be avoided? How can we introduce the child to and/or communicate the child's needs to the other children and their parents? How can the rest of the church family be supportive? Are there ways to provide respite?

It's important that all parties think of the child as God's child rather than "the child with the disability." As Uitvlugt points out, God is inclusive of all children, claiming "You are mine" at baptism and including them in the covenant promises—the role of a church family, then, is to become the tool to help facilitate what God has already put in place.

Find resources for families and churches with children who have special needs at
www.friendship.org
www.clcnetwork.org
www.faithaliveresources.org

PARENTING RESOURCES

W e asked our panel of experts to recommend helpful resources for further information on a variety of topics. Here are their suggestions:

1-2-3 Magic, developed by Dr. Thomas Phelan (Parent-Magic, Inc.)

Boundaries with Kids and *Raising Great Kids* by Dr. Henry Cloud and Dr. John Townsend (Zondervan)

Children Matter: Celebrating Their Place in the Church, Family, and Community by Scottie May, et al. (Eerdmans)

Help! I'm a Parent by S. Bruce Narramore (Zondervan)

Helping Our Children Grow in Faith: How the Church Can Nurture the Spiritual Development of Kids by Robert J. Keeley (Baker)

Just Because It's Not Wrong Doesn't Make It Right (Penguin) and *Kids Are Worth It!* (Harper) by Barbara Coloroso

Making a Home for Faith: Nurturing the Spiritual Life of Your Children by Elizabeth Caldwell (Pilgrim Press)

Parenting in the Pew by Robbie Castleman (IVP Books)

Parenting with Love and Logic by Foster Cline, M.D., and Jim Fay (NavPress)

Raising Compassionate, Courageous Children in a Violent World by Janice Cohn (Longstreet Press)

Real Kids, Real Faith: Practices for Nurturing Children's Spiritual Lives by Karen-Marie Yust (Jossey-Bass)

Siblings Without Rivalry and *How to Talk So Kids Will Listen & Listen So Kids Will Talk* by Adele Faber and Elaine Mazlish (Harper)

Teaching Kids to Care & Share by Jolene Roehlkepartain (Abingdon)

The Birth Order Book and *Have a New Kid by Friday* by Dr. Kevin Leman (Revell)

www.faithaliveresources.org

www.nurturekidsfaith.org

www.search-insititute.org

www.youthandfamilyinstitute.org (Vibrant Faith Ministries)

Special Needs Resources

A Compassionate Journey by John Cook (Faith Alive)

Acquainted with Autism by Sheila Gosney (Warner Press)

Helping Kids Include Kids with Disabilities and *Autism and Your Church* by Barbara Newman (Faith Alive)

Including People with Disabilities in Faith Communities by Erik Carter (Paul H. Brooks Pub. Co.)

Same Lake, Different Boat by Stephanie O. Hubach (P & R Press)

www.friendship.org (Friendship Ministries)

Resources for Transitional Times

Boundaries: When to Say Yes, When to Say No—To Take Control of Your Life by Dr. Henry Cloud and Dr. John Townsend (Zondervan)

Breaking the Cycle of Divorce: How Your Marriage Can Succeed Even If Your Parents' Didn't by John Trent (Tyndale House)

The Seven Principles for Making Marriage Work by John Gottman (Three Rivers Press)

Nonviolent Communication by Marshall Rosenberg (Puddledancer Press)

The Smart Step-Family by Ron L. Deal (Bethany House)

OUR PANEL OF EXPERTS

The following people have graciously shared their expertise throughout the book:

Judy Bogaart is the director of Orchard Hill Counseling Center and has her master's degree in social work. She has a private practice in Holland, Michigan.

Joyce Borger is an ordained minister in the Christian Reformed Church, editor of the quarterly journal *Reformed Worship*, and the music and worship editor for Faith Alive Christian Resources.

Celaine Bouma-Prediger is an ordained minister in the Reformed Church in America, a pastoral counselor and spiritual director, and a counselor-in-residence at Western Theological Seminary, Holland, Michigan.

Elizabeth Caldwell is the Harold Blake Walker Professor of Pastoral Theology and the associate dean for advising and formation at McCormick Theological Seminary in Chicago, Illinois. She is the author of *Making a Home for Faith: Nurturing the Spiritual Lives of Children*.

Judy Cook has a degree in psychology from Dordt College, studied family therapy at the University of Guelph, and received an M.Ed. degree in counseling from the University of Toronto. Judy worked in the family therapy field at both Christian and non-Christian agencies for twenty-five years, serving most recently as the *Salem Digest* editor and clinical director at Salem Mental Health Network.

Robert DeMoor is an ordained minister in the Christian Reformed Church; editor of *The Banner*, the magazine of the CRC; and pastor of preaching and administration for West End CRC, Edmonton, Alberta.

Marc Houck has a doctoral degree in clinical psychology from Biola University's Rosemead School of

Psychology, is affiliated with the Department of Veterans' Affairs (outpatient clinic in Grand Rapids, Michigan) and with Pine Rest Christian Mental Health Services, and is an adjunct instructor in psychology at Grand Rapids Community College.

Ron Nydam is professor of pastoral care at Calvin Theological Seminary. Prior to that he was a pastor of Third Christian Reformed Church, Denver, Colorado, and the agency director of Pastoral Counseling for Denver. Ron is the author of *Adoptees Come of Age: Living Within Two Families* and has a special interest in the study of relinquishment and adoption.

Beth A. Swagman is the director of Safe Church Ministry for the Christian Reformed Church in North America. She has a master's degree in social work and a juris doctor degree.

Jan Talen is a licensed marriage and family therapist, and owns and runs a private practice called FUNLife, LLC. (www.funlifellc.com).

Nella Uitvlugt is the executive director of Friendship Ministries and consults with churches on including children and adults with disabilities into the church education program and the full life of the church community.

Leonard Vander Zee is an ordained minister in the Christian Reformed Church. Prior to becoming the editor-in-chief and theological editor for Faith Alive Christian Resources, he was the pastor of South Bend Christian Reformed Church in Indiana.

Karen-Marie Yust is associate professor of Christian education at Union Presbyterian Seminary, an ordained minister with dual standing in the United Church of Christ and the Christian Church (Disciples of Christ), and a Christian educator. She is the author of *Real Kids, Real Faith: Practices for Nurturing Children's Spiritual Lives.*

INDEX